Sermons on *Special Occasions*

Sermons on *Special Occasions*

IAN R. K. PAISLEY

AMBASSADOR
Belfast • Greenville

Sermons *on Special Occasions*
Copyright © 1996 Ian R.K. Paisley

All rights reserved
No part of this book may be reproduced, stored in a retrieval system, or transmitted in any form or by any means - electronic, mechanical, photocopy, recording or otherwise - without written permission of the publisher, except for brief quotations in printed reviews.

ISBN 1 898787 73 5

Published by
AMBASSADOR PRODUCTIONS, LTD.
Providence House
16 Hillview Avenue,
Belfast, BT5 6JR

Emerald House
1 Chick Springs Road, Suite 102
Greenville, South Carolina, 29609

Foreword

IN MY MINISTRY OF fifty years I have been called upon to preach on many special occasions. Some of these occasions drew crowds of many thousands.

The occasion added its own excitement, emotion and exhilaration but the flesh always profiteth nothing. It was the power of the Holy Spirit alone which gave strength to the preacher and used the preaching for the exaltation of the Lord Jesus and the salvation of souls.

The Word spoken in weakness was brought forth in strength and with the sturdy Covenanter Samuel Rutherford I say that if some soul from these preachings meet me at God's right hand my heaven will be two heavens in Emmanuel's land. These sermons have not appeared in this format before. May the Master of Assemblies speed and prosper their going forth.

Yours,
"Set for the Defence of the Gospel"
Ian R.K. Paisley
Eph 6:19+20

February 1996
Martyrs Memorial Free Presbyterian Church,
356-376 Ravenhill Road,
Belfast, BT6 8GL
Northern Ireland

Contents

1. **The first sermon preached** *in the new church building* 9
   A SERMON PREACHED ON SATURDAY 4TH OCTOBER, 1969 AT THE OPENING OF THE MARTYRS MEMORIAL CHURCH.

2. **Where is the Lord God** *of Elijah?* 17
   A SERMON PREACHED TO 15,000 PEOPLE ON 18TH NOVEMBER, 1973 AT THE OPENING OF THE FOUNDERS MEMORIAL AMPHITORIUM AT BOB JONES UNIVERSITY, GREENVILLE, SOUTH CAROLINA, USA.

3. **Mary Magdalene** *at the empty tomb* 25
   A SERMON PREACHED AT AN EARLY EASTER CONVENTION GATHERING IN THE MARTYRS MEMORIAL CHURCH.

4. **The Fundamentalist** *confession* 37
   A SERMON PREACHED ON THE 32ND ANNIVERSARY OF HIS ORDINATION TO THE GOSPEL MINISTRY ON THE FIRST LORD'S DAY MORNING OF AUGUST, 1978 IN THE MARTYRS MEMORIAL CHURCH.

5. **The one and only subject** *of the Gospel* 47
   A SERMON PREACHED ON THE 45TH ANNIVERSARY OF HIS ORDINATION TO THE GOSPEL MINISTRY ON LORD'S DAY MORNING 4TH AUGUST, 1991 IN THE MARTYRS MEMORIAL CHURCH.

6. **Not ashamed** *of the Gospel* 59
   A SERMON PREACHED ON THE 45TH ANNIVERSARY OF HIS ORDINATION TO THE GOSPEL MINISTRY ON LORD'S DAY EVENING 4TH AUGUST, 1991.

7. **The Tears** *of the Minister* 69
A SERMON PREACHED ON THE 47TH ANNIVERSARY OF HIS ORDINATION TO THE GOSPEL MINISTRY ON THE FIRST LORD'S DAY MORNING OF AUGUST, 1993 IN THE MARTYRS MEMORIAL CHURCH.

8. **The Temptations** *of the Minister* 83
A SERMON PREACHED ON THE 47TH ANNIVERSARY OF HIS ORDINATION TO THE GOSPEL MINISTRY ON THE FIRST LORD'S DAY EVENING OF AUGUST, 1993 IN THE MARTYRS MEMORIAL CHURCH.

9. **World empires crash** *but God remaineth* 91
A SERMON PREACHED IN THE MARTYRS MEMORIAL CHURCH IN 1991 AFTER THE CRASH OF THE USSR AND THE RESIGNATION OF PRESIDENT GORBACHEV.

10. **The big bang** *versus the big God* 99
A SERMON PREACHED IN SEPTEMBER 1992 IN THE MARTYRS MEMORIAL CHURCH AFTER THE PRONOUNCEMENT BY SCIENTISTS THAT THE WORLD WAS CREATED BY A BIG BANG.

11. **Swearing allegiance** *to King Jesus* 113
A SERMON PREACHED ON LORD'S DAY 24TH MARCH, 1991 TO SOME 12,000 PEOPLE IN THE KINGS HALL, BELFAST ON THE 40TH ANNIVERSARY OF THE FOUNDING OF THE FREE PRESBYTERIAN CHURCH OF ULSTER.

12. **The Queen's** *Silver Jubilee* 127
A SERMON PREACHED IN 1977 IN THE MARTYRS MEMORIAL CHURCH ON THE OCCASION OF THE QUEEN'S SILVER JUBILEE.

13. **There's no place** *like Hell!* 135
A SERMON PREACHED IN 1988 IN THE MARTYRS MEMORIAL CHURCH ON THE OCCASION OF THE RESURGENCE OF THE "NO HELL THEOLOGY" AMONGST SO-CALLED EVANGELICALS.

14. **Back to** *the Cross* 143
A SERMON PREACHED ON LORD'S DAY MORNING 11TH OCTOBER, 1987 IN THE MARTYRS MEMORIAL CHURCH AND BROADCAST ON BBC RADIO ULSTER AND RADIO 4.

15. **Sixty years in Christ:** *a personal testimony* 151
A SERMON PREACHED ON 29TH MAY, 1992 IN THE MARTYRS MEMORIAL CHURCH ON THE SIXTIETH ANNIVERSARY OF HIS CONVERSION TO CHRIST.

1 The first sermon preached
in the new church building

A SERMON PREACHED ON SATURDAY 4TH OCTOBER, 1969 AT THE OPENING OF THE MARTYRS MEMORIAL CHURCH TO AN ESTIMATED CROWD OF 8,000. THE TEXT WAS HAGGAI 2:9 "THE GLORY OF THIS LATTER HOUSE SHALL BE GREATER THAN OF THE FORMER, SAITH THE LORD OF HOSTS: AND IN THIS PLACE WILL I GIVE PEACE, SAITH THE LORD OF HOSTS."
IT IS PRINTED IN ITS ORIGINAL FORM WITH LITTLE EDITING.

THIS TEXT OF HOLY Scripture can be applied in a threefold manner. First of all, it is true DISPENSATIONALLY, and I want to talk a little about its truth, viewed in this way. This text of Scripture, thank God, can be true EXPERIENTIALLY, and in a measure materially, because, praise God, we are looking forward to the glory of God filling this house in a real spiritual and marked manner. Then last of all, this text of Scripture is going to be true ETERNALLY in the future, when the first temple of God's creation is dismantled and He shakes this old world, lays it to rest and creates a new heaven and a new earth, in which dwells righteousness. Then shall it be said, as angelic voices shout eternally the praises of God, and the redeemed voices mingle with that mighty shout of triumph to the Lamb, that the glory of this latter house shall be greater than the former.

IT IS TRUE DISPENSATIONALLY

We go back to the Old Testament and we remember that the Old Testament worship was in symbols. It consisted of types, shadows, material altars and the sacrificing of the blood of animals; it consisted of something that was outward and could be handled.

But there was a day when God took down the Old Testament Tabernacle and Temple; He caused the Old Testament types to cease and brought in the glory of the latter house. Do you know Who that house was? - Jesus Christ Himself. "In the beginning was the Word and the Word was with God, and the Word was God, The same was in the beginning with God. All things were made by him; and without him was not any thing made that was made ... And the Word was made flesh, and "tabernacled", or "dwelt among us". One day, heaven's gate was opened, and there stepped out from the glory of God's eternal ages, God's Son. We dare not view Him with the natural eye but, praise God, He veiled His glory in the clay of our mortality and was made of a woman, made under the law, to redeem those that are under the law. Our eyes have seen and our hands have handled of the Word of Life. The glory of the Old Testament Tabernacle and Temple are nothing, when we behold the glory of the "only begotten of the Father, full of grace and truth."

BIBLE MIRACLES

We in this church do not question the miracles of the Bible, we believe in them; we in this church honour Christ as virgin born. If He were not, he would not have had a virgin life, He would not have had a virgin death or a virgin resurrection. There is a purity about His birth that dazzles us; there is a purity about His life that is stupendous; there is a purity about His death which is beyond human ken; there is a purity about His resurrection that staggers the infinite minds of men; and there is a purity about His coming again that is going to so radiate the world, that those who are redeemed shall share in His glory. We shall be changed in a moment in the twinkling of an eye, at the last trump. "For the dead in Christ shall rise first, and we that are alive and remain shall be caught up together with them in the air, to meet the Lord." Madam, you will be looking good then! You will not need any of the powder, paint or putty to help the face then, when God transforms you by His grace.

Let me say something from this pulpit: let me say that the grand subject of this pulpit is the uplifting of Jesus Christ, and we are going to uplift Him. We are not ashamed of the Lord Jesus.

When men come along and point their finger of scorn at His virgin birth, we shall be there to defend His virgin birth. When men come along to pour their scorn of carnal thinking and materialistic and rationalistic philosophies upon His miracles, we shall be there to defend the miraculous Christ. When men come along to disparage His blood-shedding upon the middle cross, and to say that He never rose from the tomb, we shall be there to declare that Jesus lives.

"You ask me how I know He lives,
He lives within my heart!"

This edifice today is a testimony that Jesus lives, that Jesus leads and that Jesus is coming again.

There are three things about this text DISPENSATIONALLY. The glory of this latter house shall be greater than the former, because of

THE FINALITY OF HIS PRIESTHOOD

Under the Old Testament economy, the priest died and another took his place. The priest needed to come often to the altar to offer many sacrifices for sins that the writer to the Hebrews, Paul, tells us, could never put away sins.

But, praise God, there has come among us our glorious, great High Priest. "Who is He that cometh from Edom with dyed garment from Bozrah? He that is glorious in His apparel - mighty to save." I see upon His garments the sweat and blood of Gethsemane. I see upon His garments the marks of cruel suffering, for they tore the garments from off His back, and He withheld not Himself from shame. And, in yonder glory today there is One Who wears His vesture dipped in blood, and His Name is the Word of God.

Who is He, this priest Who put all other priesthoods away? This Priest is Jesus Christ! Let me tell you today that there is power in the nail-pierced hands of this Priest to forgive you. Let me tell you that from the lips of this Priest there is a word of pardon that can transform your life. Let me tell you that in the hem of this Priest's garment - and the hem is the finished work - there is life for you.

She only touched the hem of His garment
As to His side she stole;
Amid the crowd that gather around Him
And straightaway she was whole.
Oh touch the hem of His garment
And thou too shalt be free ;
Its saving power, this very hour
Shall give new life to thee.

The priesthoods of man have passed away and there stands before God a great High Priest. "This man, having offered one sacrifice for sins for ever, sat down at the right hand of God. That is the glory of THE FINALITY OF HIS PRIESTHOOD."

THE VITALITY OF ITS PROCLAMATION

We have a message that transforms, we have a Christ that really saves. This church is not going to be a morgue. Thank God for that!

Mr. Nicholson used to say, in his own way, that if you brought a bucket of milk through the door of some churches, before you got it to the pulpit, it would be buttermilk!

I want to say that this church will be warm, because our hearts will be warmed by the Gospel of Jesus Christ. We have come here today into this house, to make it a sanctuary, the gate of Heaven. The doors of this church will be open to all who shall come.

We are glad that among the crowd today there are many Roman Catholics whom I know, who asked me personally if they could come. They are here today and we are glad that they are here.

NEED OF ALL MEN

This church does not believe that because a man is a Protestant he is going to Heaven; this church believes that except a man be born again, whether he be a Protestant or a Roman Catholic, whether he be an Hibernian or an Orangeman, whether he be good living in the terms of men, or evil living in the terms of men, he needs to be radically and eternally transformed by the Spirit of God. This is the thing that this church stands for.

Of course, the press will not tell you that. They will tell you that this is the place where Paisley sharpens his sword to get at the Roman Catholics. Don't you believe that! We have every respect for every individual, we have no respect at all for the system of Romanism. We have less respect for the system of apostate Protestantism that has robbed the Bible of its inspiration, the Blood of its power and the Christ of His Name. Let me say that with all my heart. We have got a Bible message.

I will tell you about Joe Black. I came to the Ravenhill Road twenty-three years ago. We had an open air meeting at the end of the park and I saw Joe, overcome with booze, pulling his way along the railings of the park. I went over to him, put my hand on his shoulders and said, "I have a message for you." "For me?" he asked, "Yes," I said, "for you. Jesus Christ loves you." He replied, "Nobody loves me. You don't know who you are talking to." I said, "I do. What about coming down to the wee church at Shamrock Street and we will talk there?" He answered, "I couldn't reach it. I can't walk because I'm overcome with booze. Smell my breath." I picked him up and carried him. They always thought that I was a fool on this road, so I might as well live up to the reputation. I carried Joe into that small church and we knelt down together and I led Joe Black to Jesus. That's many years ago. He never went back to booze and never will - for God saved him.

I could spend a long time telling you of thousands of men in the same condition, some high in rank. Not so long ago, one of the biggest business men in this city, found himself at the door of my house at 1.30 in the morning after the Lord's Day. He told me that he had gone to the Ulster Hall to mock and curse me, but said, "I found something there that I can't escape from. Would you lead me to Jesus?" I had the great joy of leading him to Christ.

BIBLE MESSAGE

We have a Bible message - a message that is living, and if you have come here today and are sitting here, or in the tents, or listening outside in the road and your heart is sore; if you have a burden that nobody knows about; if you have trouble that no one can share and you have a chain around your spirit that is drawing and cutting you to the very quick - praise God, my Saviour can lift your burden. My Saviour can break your chains - His Blood can make ten thousand clean, His blood avails for you.

Our message is a Bible message, and we are going to preach it and rejoice, because God has given us the opportunity, in this magnificent building, to fill the seats and proclaim this message. This church is going to be the cradle of a great revival. I do not say that flippantly. I say it because many years ago, on my knees in my old church, God promised to send a revival through my ministry and I am waiting for and expecting that great day of blessing. May God speed the day when the clouds will break and there will be blessing so that there will not be room enough to receive it.

THE ETERNITY OF ITS PEACE

This is the glory of the latter house - peace. We met a news-man from Eire Television the other day and he said. "What contribution are you going to make to peace?" I said to him, "We are going to make the best possible contribution towards peace - we are going to preach the Gospel of Jesus Christ." Amongst all troubles, perplexities, heartaches and headaches that we have to face as we saunter along the pilgrim way of life's crooked and rugged road, Jesus Christ can give you peace.

I can testify that during my twenty-three years of ministry, God has given me perfect peace. There is no preacher more maligned than I am, I am not sobbing about it. I am rejoicing that God can keep in the midst of the tempest. God can keep you in the midst of His love. They have had debates in Stormont, Westminster, and the UNO Do you think that those things annoy me? I ate three meals a day when they debated, and I slept well at night. I have read things in the newspapers about me that I did not even know! I have been in prison twice for my principles. I have mingled with murderers and with those fallen down into the troughs of sin. They are no worse than you were, only God received you, friend. I worked for weeks with men who were of the criminal class and I was locked in my cell for hours on end.

I can testify today that Jesus gives peace. I walked in the valley of the shadows when my life was threatened and an attempt was made to poison me by one who was an emissary of the Roman Catholic Church. When I lay on my bed and the doctor shook his head, thinking that it was the end, down there lingering in the valley, I knew the peace of God, a peace that the sons of this world can never know. You know what my prayer is? That you will get peace today. You need peace; you need strength; you need help.

GOD WILL FULFIL THIS ETERNALLY

This is what this church is heading for - the coming of our great God and Saviour Jesus Christ. There is a day when the apocalyptic vision of John is going to be fulfilled. 'I saw a new heaven and a new earth for the former things are passed away.'

This old earth is a glorious place. It is nice to rise in the morning and see the sun rise to run its race. It is nice to rise at night, to stand under the starry heavens and see God's handiwork. 'The heavens declare the glory of God and the firmament showeth His handiwork'.

There is a day when these eyes of mine, in a glorified body, are going to look into a new heaven and that new heaven is going to far exceed the old creation. We are going to walk the new earth. Praise God, we are all going to be changed. The body will have no more pain there. No blight of the sorrows of death will be on the hillsides of the new heaven and the new earth; death is unknown there. There will be no more sea - sea speaks of separation and, praise God, there will be no more separation.

You know when we come to a day like this, we say, 'Lord build us three tabernacles and let us stay here,' but we have got to go down into the valley and fight. Praise God, some day I will fight my last battle, some day I will preach my last sermon. I hope it is not going to be for a long time, for there are a few people I want to clean up before I come to that!

I feel like Joshua. You remember Joshua was having a great battle and there was only one thing worrying him, like a preacher, it was the clock!

The sun was sinking, and he wanted to really beat the enemy. He said, 'Sun, stand still.' Many times I have prayed that prayer and have said, 'Lord, let the sun of my ministry stand still so that I can really use the sword on these apostates and press the battle to the gates.' Praise God, there they leave down their sword, they hang their shields upon the walls and they learn the rules of war no more.

There is a day when, robed in the immaculate white robes that have been washed in the blood that flowed from Immanuel's veins, we, the redeemed of the Lord, shall enter into a city that hath foundations, whose builder and maker is God. The streets of that city are pure gold and the walls are of jasper.

Let me tell you, I see no temple therein, for the Lord God and the Lamb are the temple thereof. The Lamb is all the glory in Immanuel's Land.

> 'With mercy and with judgment
> My web of time He wove;
> And aye the dews of sorrow
> Were lustred with His love;,
> I'll bless the hand that guided,
> I'll bless the heart that planned,
> When throned where glory dwelleth
> In Immanuel's Land.'

Will you be there, friend? That is the important question.

> *'I'm going home to glory soon,*
> *To see the city bright;*
> *To walk the golden streets of heaven*
> *And bask in God's own light.*
> *But some of you are out of Christ,*
> *And held by many a snare;*
> *I cannot leave you lost and lone,*
> *I want you over there.'*

May we all, by the grace of God, know Jesus Christ as our Saviour and as our friend.

Amen and Amen

2 Where is the Lord God *of Elijah?*

A SERMON PREACHED TO 15,000 PEOPLE ON 18TH NOVEMBER, 1973 AT THE OPENING OF THE FOUNDERS MEMORIAL AMPHITORIUM AT BOB JONES UNIVERSITY, GREENVILLE, SOUTH CAROLINA, USA.

CHANCELLOR JONES, DR JONES, distinguished guests and all who have come to listen to God's Word today, I would like to sincerely say what a great honour it is for me to be the first to preach in this great building. I trust that we will have the anointing of the Holy Spirit upon His word as we seek to uplift the revealed truth of the gospel of Jesus Christ.

I am glad that Dr Jones Snr came of Ulster stock, so we in Ulster can take credit for some of the great things which have been accomplished through his ministry and the great school that he founded.

I am reading the Word of God from the 18th chapter of the first book of Kings at verse 7 "And as Obadiah was in the way, behold, Elijah met him: and he knew him, and fell on his face, and said, Art thou that my lord Elijah? And he answered him, I am: go, tell thy lord, Behold, Elijah is here. And he said, What have I sinned, that thou wouldest deliver thy servant into the hand of Ahab, to slay me? As the Lord thy God liveth, there is no nation or kingdom, whither my lord hath not sent to seek thee: and when they said, He is not there; he took an oath of the kingdom and nation, that they found thee not. And now behold thou sayest, Go tell thy lord, Behold Elijah is here. And it shall come to pass, as soon as

I am gone from thee, that the Spirit of the Lord shall carry thee whither I know not; and so when I come and tell Ahab, and he cannot find thee, he shall slay me: but I thy servant fear the Lord from my youth. Was it not told my lord what I did when Jezebel slew the prophets of the Lord, how I hid an hundred men of the Lord's prophets by fifty in a cave, and fed them with bread and water? And now thou sayest, Go, tell thy lord, Behold, Elijah is here: and he shall slay me. And Elijah said, As the Lord of hosts liveth, before whom I stand, I will surely shew myself unto him today." God shall stamp with His own Divine seal of approval and blessing this reading from the infallible Book.

In every age God has His Elijahs. These Elijahs plough an individual and unique furrow as far as the church of God is concerned. They are unusual men, characterised by an Elijah-like ministry with its peculiarities and with its special powers. They are not of the common mould and it can be said that after their making God breaks the mould so that there will never again be another. Such a man was Dr Bob Jones Snr. His like will never be seen again.

In this great and unusual building erected to his memory, it is fitting that today we should magnify the grace of God that made Bob Jones what he was in the cause of Christ and in the kingdom of our Lord Jesus. He would not desire that any glory should be given to him but that all the glory should be the Lord's.

A visitor went to St Paul's cathedral and asked one of the guides "Where is the memorial to the architect of the cathedral, Sir Christopher Wren?" The guide replied "Look around you." We could well say today "What is the memorial to the life and the ministry and the work of Dr Bob Jones?" Just look around you. I am not referring today to this wonderful building or to the other buildings on the campus of this unique university, but I say, go to the fundamentalist pulpits in your country and there you will see men preaching under the anointing of the Holy Spirit of God the great and glorious news of the gospel of Christ, defending the faith, contending in an evil age against apostasy for the Crown rights of King Jesus and the Crown jewels of His glorious gospel and there you will see the work and the ministry of the founder of this great school. Go to the mission fields of the world where faithful missionaries are presenting, not the manufactured philosophies of man, but the great truths revealed in Holy Scripture concerning the glorious Person and the Work of God's dear Son. As you view those missionaries who have gone forth there you have the memorial to the founder of this great school.

It can be well said that God has a man for the hour and an hour for the man. God had Bob Jones for an hour in the history of your great country and he was revealed at the right time by the power of the Spirit of God to do the work that God had specially chosen him to do.

If you look with me at the chapter which we were reading you will notice in verses eight, eleven and fourteen, these great words, "Behold Elijah is here". What was said of Elijah could be said of all the great leaders in the history of the Christian church. In Geneva it could be said, "Behold John Calvin in here." In the northern kingdom of Scotland it could be said, "Behold John Knox is here." In London it could be said, "Behold Bishop Latimer is here" and in a unique sense in the great land that you love and have a right to love, it could be said in the history of the church in America, "Behold Bob Jones is here." He came on the American scene at the right time, for it was God's time. He came with the right message, because he was a man endued with power from on high. He stood fearlessly and forcibly for the great truths of the gospel. Today we thank God for him, and one day we will bless God with him.

I always give an outline when I am preaching. I never finish it, but I always have one anyway. I want to leave with you five thoughts on this text which I have chosen.

First of all, Behold Elijah is here as the man of God's choice. Secondly, Behold Elijah is here as the man from God's crucible. Thirdly, Behold Elijah is here as the man reflecting God's character. Fourthly, Behold Elijah is here as the man under God's commission. Fifthly and lastly, Behold Elijah is here as the man with God's challenge.

ELIJAH, THE MAN OF GOD'S CHOICE

Let us look at the first one - Behold Elijah is here as the man of God's choice. In a day of national apostasy and deep spiritual declension, when the altars of the true God were broken down and the altars of the false god, Baal, were erected, when the priests of Israel had become corrupted and the Royal House of Israel had become totally and absolutely corrupted through Queen Jezebel and her consort Ahab, God raised up a man called Elijah. Elijah means *Jehovah is my God*. So everywhere he went his very name was a testimony against the corruption and the idolatry and apostasy of his day. The nation said "Baal is my god," Elijah said "Jehovah is my God." He was a man chosen of God to do a great task in an evil age and in an idolatrous situation. He was a man chosen of God for that task. Behold Elijah is here as the man of God's choice.

There is a name synonymous with the history of fundamentalism in the United States of America and across the world today and that is the name of Bob Jones. God chose this man in an evil age, in a day of declension, in a time of apostasy, to raise up the bloodstained banner of the cross, to preach the great truths of the Bible. Dr Jones was a tremendous preacher of the Word of God. He used to say "Make way for the gospel train." He believed in the power of the preaching of God's Word.

Every revival in church history was a revival of great preaching. The church of Jesus Christ has gone cold and formal and has become corrupt and apostate when the pulpit has been weak and the preacher has been weak. In the modern ecumenical age the pulpit is pushed to the side because preaching is only a sideline in the ecumencial church but in the churches that stand for Reformation truth the pulpit has the pre-eminence and upon the desk is the open Word of God, the infallible scriptures, and behind the desk is someone who believes that God has one method divinely ordained for the salvation of souls and that is the preaching of the cross. "For the preaching of the cross is to them that perish foolishness but unto us who are saved it is the power of God." Thank God today Bob Jones is here. He is here because his influence lives on today. His glorified spirit is in heaven. His body rests in the little island awaiting the trumpet of the first resurrection but his influence lives on today as a man who was chosen of the Lord. How we rejoice that God looked down from heaven and chose this man in your country to be the great champion, the great leader, the great protagonist of the gospel of Jesus Christ. Today we bless God for his memory and for hia work.

ELIJAH, THE MAN FROM GOD'S CRUCIBLE

Secondly, Behold Elijah is here, the man from God's crucible. Gold must be tried by fire. It must be proved in the furnace. The true prophet of God comes forth through the testing fires of temptation. No man of God can ever have peculiar and special power until he has drunk the cup of testing and until he has partaken of deep sorrow and trial. It is the way of the cross practised and known in the life of the preacher that gives him power. Elijah sat down by the brook and slowly but surely he saw that brook drying up. Every morning he slaked his thirst at that brook. Every evening he again refreshed himself with its waters but slowly, surely and steadily the brook was drying up. Did you ever sit in imagination with Elijah and watch that brook as it dried up? The thing that supported him was now going to support him no longer. The thing that he depended upon was slowly and surely being taken away from him. Elijah was thrown back upon God Himself. God took the faith of the prophet from the means and put the faith of the prophet in the One who supplies the means. In his ministry Dr Jones knew what it was to see the means that helped him in his ministry dry up, but the God of heaven never failed. When the battles became fierce, men who once stood with him quivered, and some went back and walked no more with him, but the man of God went forward because he was being tested in the crucible of affliction. It was because of that testing, it was because of that Gethsemane experience that the servant of God was moulded into the great leader that he became in the Christian church.

Elijah stood in the home of death. He looked down upon the body of the little son and his heart was sore. Dr Jones was a man who knew something of life's sorrow, who had tasted of life's trials, who endured affliction as a good soldier of Jesus Christ but he came forth from the fire burnished, more than ever fitted to wield the sword of the gospel and unfurl the banner of truth and righteousness. Behold Elijah is here as the man from God's crucible.

ELIJAH, THE MAN REFLECTING GOD'S CHARACTER

Thirdly, Behold Elijah is here as the man reflecting God's character. Elijah was burned up with jealousy for the Lord of Hosts. When he walked through the country and saw the groves of the Baal worshippers, and the altars to the false gods, and the corruption of the priests, and the deflection of Israel from the commandments of Jehovah, his heart burned with fiery indignation. His mouth was open to declare the judgment of God upon sin and upon all that sin does in its cancerous power in the community

He reflected in that indignation the fiery indignation of the God who had sent him. He was jealous for the Lord of Hosts. In the character of Dr Bob Jones there was a reflection of the very character of God Himself. When the Westminster Assembly of Divines (this will do the Baptists good who are here) were drawing up their great doctrinal statement and their shorter catechism they came to the study of the question - "Who is God?" They wondered how they would answer in their catechism that vital question. They called upon the youngest member of that august Assembly, George Gillespie, a young minister from Scotland's

Kirk to lead in prayer. When George Gillespie stood up he quoted the words of the Lord Jesus, "God is a Spirit", and he went on to say, "infinite, eternal and unchangeable, in His being, wisdom, power, holiness, justice, goodness and truth."

The man of God will reflect the character of the God whom he serves. In Dr Bob Jones we had wisdom. Those of you who sat at his feet are well aware of the proverbial wisdom that came forth from his heart. I met him on just one occasion. I will never forget that meeting when he laid his hands very lovingly and graciously upon my shoulders and he said this to me, "Orthodoxy cannot function without evangelistic unction." That is true. That is the wisdom of God. You folks know some of the other great sayings of the founder of this school. He was a man with wisdom. Why? Because he walked with the God of wisdom.

What this nation needs today is a race of wise men who have the wisdom of God. The philosophies of this modern age will not save your nation and my nation from sinking down into hell, but the gospel of Christ will save the nation. God send us preachers of the gospel of Christ, for Christ is the power of God and Christ is the wisdom of God.

Let us take the second attribute, power. Dr Jones was dynamic in his ministry. You did not go to sleep when he preached the Word. I am reminded of the story of an old Scottish preacher by the name of Dr Kydd, from Aberdeen. He was preaching one summer's evening to a packed church, the atmosphere was heavy and he saw one of his congregation close his eyes and fall asleep. The old preacher stopped, called him by his name and said, "William, waken up." So William rubbed his eyes, looked up at the preacher and the preacher continued his message. Later in the service William again went to sleep. So the old preacher took the Bible and threw it down and hit him on the head and said, "If you will not hear the Word by the grace of God you will feel it."

Those that listened to Dr Jones felt the power of the Word of God. Thank God there is power in this Book and we believe it with all our hearts. The preaching of this Book can turn the tide in an apostate day. The preaching of this Book can call men from the outer darkness of their sin into the glorious light and immortality of the gospel. This Book can take you from the fearful pit and from the miry clay and set your feet upon the Rock and establish your way. He had power. We need power in the pulpit today. We need men of power.

Holiness. This campus stands for scriptural holiness. When you walk on to this campus you can see in the dress of the students a reflection of chastity and purity. Thank God for it. In an age that is permissive, in an age that is immoral, in an age that is exceedingly lustful and sinful thank God for the standards of this university. They are Christian standards. They are the standards to which Christian people should adhere. Our brother set himself against all conformity to the world and he was against compromise in every shape and form.

Justice. What man in America stood more for justice than Dr Jones?

Goodness. He was a man great in heart. His goodness reached out after all his students and after all his hearers. When he looked at a person he did not look upon them as another member of society but he looked at them as a soul whom Christ died to save and a soul with potential and talents for the extension of the Kingdom of God on earth.

Truth. He was a great defender of the truth. In this school which he founded and the heritage which he left, is a heritage in defence of the truth. "Ye shall know the truth," said the Lord Jesus Christ, "and the truth shall set you free." Behold Elijah is here as the man reflecting God's character.

ELIJAH, THE MAN UNDER GOD'S COMMISSION

Fourthly, Behold Elijah is here as a man under God's commission. Elijah was under marching orders from heaven. When you have got your marching orders from heaven you do not fear man, woman or devil. When God commands it is onward and forward. So it was with Elijah. He cared not how great the opposition. God had ordered him to walk this way and he must walk this way. Dr Jones was a man who knew discipline in his own life and because of that he expected to see discipline in the lives of his students. He himself practised Christian obedience so he expected God's people not to be disobedient to the heavenly vision. His whole life was motivated and controlled and dominated by the fact that he was under marching orders from heaven. When Christ said "Advance," no matter what the opposition may be, then advance it must be. There must be no turning back. There must be no half measures. There must be no half-hearted activity. It must be all in the call that Jesus Christ had ordered.

ELIJAH, THE MAN WITH GOD'S CHALLENGE

Finally, Elijah is here as the man with God's challenge. Elijah challenged the whole nation. He challenged the nation that was religiously corrupt. He challenged the nation that was morally corrupt. He challenged the nation that was educationally corrupt. So did God's honoured servant challenge this nation. He made the pulpit his throne. He made this Book the law of his life. When he stood to preach he had the command and the authority of the God of heaven, and as he fought the forces of antichrist and the forces of corruption he fought as Elijah fought, for celestial fire burned within his soul. He knew his dawn. He had been often in the secret place. He was no stranger to communion with the Most High. God took Elijah home. His mantle fell upon Elisha. You remember the first words of Elisha when he was challenged with the running Jordan before him. He said, "Where is the Lord God of Elijah?" The waters were parted and Elisha went over dry shod. You can ask today where is the Lord God of Bob Jones? Thank God He is with us today. God's honoured servant is gone but the mantle has fallen upon his son and upon his grandson and upon those associated with them. Praise God as long as this school stands for the gospel of Christ the God of heaven will stand by this school. Whether Government or President or Kings turn against it God will vindicate it and the Lord of heaven will delight his soul within it.

When the Lieutenant Governor made me welcome today I said to Dr Jones that it reminded me of the day when the Lieutenant Governor of the Crumlin Road Jail welcomed me to prison. He did not say what the Governor said here today, "Be at home." No, he did not say that to me. When I arrived in jail I was not at home, I was far from home. Let me say today dynasties may fall, governments may come and go, the flood of Jordan may ebb or flow in full spate but the God of heaven still lives and the God that answers by fire, let Him be the God! Elijah's God still lives today to take the guilt of sin away, and when I cry in Jesus' name, He answers still by fire.

May this pulpit be the sounding board of Jesus Christ and Him crucified. May it be written in the Lamb's Book of Life in this building that man and that woman was born here. May this school go forward under the commands of the great Captain of our salvation, Jesus Christ Himself, and when our task on earth is done, when the battle cries are over, and when the great church militant becomes the church triumphant, there on the glory shore with the beloved founder of this great school, we shall stand together and sing "Worthy is the Lamb, for the Lamb is all the glory in Immanuel's Land."

God bless you.

Amen and Amen

3 Mary Magdalene
at the empty tomb

A SERMON PREACHED AT AN EARLY EASTER CONVENTION GATHERING IN THE MARTYRS MEMORIAL CHURCH. THE TEXT WAS JOHN 20:11-18 "BUT MARY STOOD WITHOUT AT THE SEPULCHRE WEEPING: AND AS SHE WEPT, SHE STOOPED DOWN, AND LOOKED INTO THE SEPULCHRE, AND SEETH TWO ANGELS IN WHITE SITTING, THE ONE AT THE HEAD, AND THE OTHER AT THE FEET, WHERE THE BODY OF JESUS HAD LAIN. AND THEY SAY UNTO HER, WOMAN, WHY WEEPEST THOU? SHE SAITH UNTO THEM, BECAUSE THEY HAVE TAKEN AWAY MY LORD, AND I KNOW NOT WHERE THEY HAVE LAID HIM. AND WHEN SHE HAD THUS SAID, SHE TURNED HERSELF BACK, AND SAW JESUS STANDING, AND KNEW NOT THAT IT WAS JESUS. JESUS SAITH UNTO HER, WOMAN, WHY WEEPEST THOU? WHOM SEEKEST THOU? SHE, SUPPOSING HIM TO BE THE GARDENER, SAITH UNTO HIM, SIR, IF THOU HAVE BORNE HIM HENCE, TELL ME WHERE THOU HAST LAID HIM, AND I WILL TAKE HIM AWAY. JESUS SAITH UNTO HER, MARY. SHE TURNED HERSELF AND SAITH UNTO HIM, RAB-BO-NI; WHICH IS TO SAY, MASTER. JESUS SAITH UNTO HER, TOUCH ME NOT; FOR I AM NOT YET ASCENDED TO MY FATHER: BUT GO TO MY BRETHREN, AND SAY UNTO THEM, I ASCEND UNTO MY FATHER, AND YOUR FATHER; AND TO MY GOD, AND YOUR GOD. MARY MAGDALENE CAME AND TOLD THE DISCIPLES THAT SHE HAD SEEN THE LORD, AND THAT HE HAD SPOKEN THESE THINGS UNTO HER."

I WANT TO SPEAK UPON Mary Magdalene and the Lord's resurrection and especially her part at the sepulchre as the first person to see the risen Christ.

By way of preface could I say that there is great danger of making too much of one aspect of Christian truth to the undervaluing of other equally important aspects. A wrong emphasis prepares the way to wrong doctrine. A wrong emphasis can turn doctrine into dogma.

While too much can never be made of the death of the Lord Jesus Christ, yet in the church today too little is being made of our Lord's resurrection. I believe that we need to reinforce and reaffirm and redeclare the great doctrine of the resurrection of the Lord Jesus Christ from Joseph's tomb.

NEW TESTAMENT TEACHING

Let me show you some scripture which will underscore and underline this. I Corinthians chapter fifteen: This is a very important chapter! I want you to notice that this chapter gives us a definition of the gospel of Jesus Christ: "Moreover, brethren, I declare unto you the gospel which I preached unto you, which also ye have received," (He did not say 'which I read unto you'. He did not have a manuscript and read a sermon. He was a preacher!) "and wherein you stand: By which also ye are saved, if ye keep in memory what I preached unto you, unless ye have believed in vain. For I delivered unto you first of all that which I also received," (There is the divine origin of the gospel) "how that Christ died for our sins according to the scriptures;" (There is the authority of the gospel, it is according to the scriptures) "how that Christ died for our sins" (There is the atonement of the gospel) "And that He was buried, and that He rose again the third day according to the scriptures." (There is the dynamic of the gospel.) So in the great substance, the great kernel and in the great sweep of the gospel the resurrection of Christ is placed on a par with the divine origin of the gospel, the divine authority of the gospel and with the atoning death upon the Cross.

Turn in your Bible to Romans chapter four and verse twenty-five and we read there these words: "Who was delivered for our offences, and was raised again for our justification."

"Who was delivered." That is, the Lord Jesus Christ was delivered to death for our offences. "And was raised again for our justification" and the word "for" is, of course, emphasising the reason for it. He was delivered because of. The reason for His death was "our offences". The reason for His resurrection was "our justification". What does that mean? That means that Jesus could not have risen from the dead except the full price of sin had been paid. Jesus said, "It is finished." Nothing needed to be added to it. Because He paid it all He rose from the dead. You see sin would still have a mortgage on His body in the tomb if He had not discharged the whole debt. Jesus having discharged the whole debt, neither death nor sin nor the Devil could hold Him in the tomb. He was raised again because of our justification.

Turn to I Corinthians 15:14 and you will find that we have no gospel, no faith, no salvation except Christ be risen from the dead. I Corinthians fifteen and verse fourteen: "And if Christ be not risen, then is our preaching vain, and your faith is also vain." No resurrection, no salvation, no faith, no gospel preaching of Truth! So the resurrection is the very keystone of the gospel.

Turn to Acts chapter one and verse twenty-two (and we are only glancing at these verses. You can mark them and study them.) The credentials of apostleship, and one of the essentials to be an apostle was to be a witness of the resurrection. Acts 1:22 "Beginning from the baptism of John, unto that same day that He was taken up from us, must one be ordained to be a witness with us (of what?) His resurrection." Of course, if you read a little further in the Book of the Acts you will find that in verse thirty-three of chapter four the statement "And with great power gave the apostles witness of the resurrection." So the resurrection must start on an equal par with the death of the Saviour.

OLD TESTAMENT TYPES

If you glance at the Old Testament scriptures you will find there are many types of the resurrection. The resurrection is first of all suggested to us in Genesis 3:15. Because in Genesis 3:15 we have the prophecy of the absolute victory of Christ over the serpent. The serpent's head was to be bruised.

Jesus Christ proved that He had bruised the serpent's head. How? By rising from the dead and showing that He had destroyed him that had the power of death, that is to say the Devil.

You have another wondrous type of the resurrection in Genesis with Isaac. Isaac was laid on the altar after three days journey. And if you read Hebrews chapter eleven and verse nineteen you will find that Paul says he was a type of the resurrection. Abraham received Isaac back from the dead as in a figure. It was after three days and three nights.

I was greatly struck this week when I discovered that the children of Israel marched into the Red Sea exactly three days and three nights after the Passover lamb was slain. And of course the Red Sea crossing is a perfect type of the resurrection. They went down into death and they rose again three days and three nights after they had eaten the Passover lamb.

CONTRAST OF LAZARUS AND THE LORD

Joseph is a great type of the resurrection when he was in prison. In Joseph you have the prefiguration and prophetic anticipation of Christ leaving His grave clothes in the tomb. You know if you read the scriptures you would discover his garments. He left his prison clothes in prison. When Jesus Christ came out of the grave He was not like Lazarus. You know there is a great difference between Lazarus and the Lord Jesus Christ. Human hands rolled away the stone from Lazarus's grave. Angelic hands rolled away the stone from the Lord's grave. Lazarus came out dressed in the garments of death. Jesus came out having left the death rags behind Him, and He came out in all the glory of His resurrection power. Lazarus came out of the tomb to go back into the tomb some say but Jesus Christ will never die! His entombment is once and for all. His enthronement is once and for all. "I am He that liveth and was dead, and behold I am alive for evermore." Notice the difference. "That in all things the Lord Jesus Christ might have the pre-eminence."

NO HUMAN EYE SAW CHRIST RISE

I want you to notice something. No human eye actually saw the resurrection of the Lord Jesus Christ. No human eye actually saw the death of the Lord Jesus Christ, because there was a blanket of darkness laid around the cross. When it pleased the Lord to bruise His Son after all that man had done, when God took in hand the chastening of my blessed Saviour for me, no human eye saw it. When they came to examine Him He was dead already. No human eye saw Him die.

No human eye saw Him rise from the tomb. For those things are not given for human eyes to see or for human eyes to behold. But, praise God, the eye of faith has seen Him die, and the eye of faith has seen Him live, and the eye of faith beholds Him now in the everlasting Throne of God.

WOMEN RULED OUT

Something else I want to tell you. No woman under the Mosaic law was allowed to be a witness. She was never called to court, never allowed to witness about anything. I do not know whether the Mosaic law propounded the great theory that a woman's word would be so influenced by emotions and other considerations that she would not give accurate witness.

That is why in I Corinthians fifteen there is no mention of any woman as a witness to the resurrection. You go down that chapter and you will not get the mention of any woman, it is limited to the brethren only. They are not Plymouth Brethren either they are the Lord's brethren! Free Presbyterians rightly included! Amen! And the Plymouth Brethren of course not left out!

THE SIGNIFICANCE OF THE NUMBERS

Let me tell you something else about the resurrection. If you study the scriptures you will find that the Lord Jesus Christ had eleven witnesses to His resurrection before He ascended to Heaven. Eleven times He made His appearance before He ascended to Heaven. Three times after he ascended to Heaven the resurrected Christ was seen again. He was seen of Stephen at his martyrdom: Stephen saw the Son of God standing at the right hand of the Father. He was seen of Paul on the Damascus road. He was seen of John in the Isle of Patmos. Now if you multiply seven and two together you get fourteen. The Holy Ghost has His numbers right. For two in scripture is the number of witness. Seven in scripture is the number of perfection. And seven multiplied by two makes fourteen. So fourteen is the perfect witness of the resurrection of the Lord Jesus Christ.

There is going to be another witness of the resurrection. Every believer, at His Coming, is going to witness the resurrected Christ. So if you add one to fourteen you get fifteen. And fifteen is a great number. Five is the number of grace, three is the number of completion. If you multiply five by three you get fifteen which is complete grace.

Thank God, some day by grace complete we will see Him face to face and tell the story saved by grace.

Now that is just the preface to my sermon. I have not started to preach yet!

The Lord's resurrection is a great subject, and this woman Mary Magdalene is a wonderful person. We will only be able to take a limited look at it this morning.

Keep in mind three words when you read John's gospel chapter twenty. First of all the word "quest" for it started off with Mary's quest.

The second word is "request" because in this chapter there are three requests. There is Mary's request. There is the angel's request. There is the Lord's request.

Then it finished with "bequest". And the Lord gave to Mary three blessed things which we are going to look at.

FIRST: THE QUEST

Could I say something to you. There is a difference between Matthew, Luke and John.

John's gospel is the gospel of the individual. That is why in the first chapter you have the individual conversation between the Lord and Peter. And Peter gets his name changed. He was Simon and he is now Peter. And he is not called a Rock as the modern perversions put it. He was called a stone. When he wrote his epistle he remembered that and he said: "Ye also as living stones." In John chapter one you have another personal interview between Nathaniel and the Lord. In chapter three you have an individual conversation between the Lord and Nicodemus. In chapter four you have another conversation between the Lord and the woman at the well.

John's gospel is filled with individual transactions.

Now Mary Magdalene did not go to the sepulchre alone. She went in company. The company are not mentioned by John. John is the gospel of the individual. But there is no contradiction you know. If you read the scriptures carefully you will find that all the narratives dovetail together in perfect harmony. Some critics say "How can you reconcile the women going and then Mary Magdalene going on her own?" It is quite simple! Mary Magdalene did not wait. When she saw the open tomb she ran to tell the disciples and when she came back again the other women had gone. She was there on her own! It is quite simple if you read and study it correctly.

A COURAGEOUS QUEST

Let us look at it. The first thing I want to say about her quest is this. It was a courageous quest. She went in the dark. She knew there were Roman soldiers at the sepulchre. She also, as she made her way, heard the great earthquake when the angel came down and rolled away the stone. Here is this frail trembling woman and yet she is courageous enough to make the quest. Do you know all she was going for? It says "she was going to see the tomb." She was going to see the place of death and yet she was courageous enough to make this quest.

A ZEALOUS QUEST

The second thing about it, it was a zealous quest. She got up early in the morning. (And that is what you have got to do this week at the prayer meetings. Get up early in the morning!) I will give you a verse for this week of prayer. It is a verse that has been a real blessing to my soul: Proverbs 8:17 And I will tell you what to do this week. Before you go to bed read this verse and when you wake up in the morning read it again, it will encourage you. And I am sure this verse covers the case of Mary Magdalene. What does it say? "I love them that love me; and those that seek me early shall find me." That is the Word of the Lord. Mary Magdalene loved her Lord; she sought Him early. It was a zealous quest.

A LOVING QUEST

Could I also mention that it was a loving quest. If you read the gospels you will find that Mary was the last woman to behold the shut tomb. It says in Matthew's gospel that she sat watching them burying the Lord. She took her seat and sat down and watched the burial and the entombment of the body of Christ. She did not get much sleep that night. I do not believe that Mary slept at all. She waited. She could not wait until the sun rose, so she went out while it was yet dark towards the dawning of the day, and her heart was filled and she said, "Oh, that I might go and look on the place where they have laid my Lord." "Let me like Mary through the gloom come with a gift for Thee, show to me now the empty tomb, lead me to Calvary." Her heart was filled with love! I bemoan the fact of my own lovelessness to the Saviour. How much we should love Him and seek after Him with all our hearts, and with all our souls and with all our minds.

A MISGUIDED QUEST

There is something else about her quest. It was totally misguided. Although it was zealous and courageous and loving it was misguided. She was come seeking the living among the dead. You know the words she spoke are really a contradiction. She said to Peter and John: "They have taken away the Lord." If He was the Lord He was the Lord of death. If He was the Lord He was the conqueror of the tomb. But it did not dawn on her when she called Him Lord that she was misguided in thinking that somebody had taken Him away. Do you know what she did? The first time she ran to tell the apostles her false assumption, and the second time she was a carrier of the truth. (The first time she ran to tell Peter and John. There is a lovely little thought here: John must have taken Peter to his own home. He did not forsake Peter when Peter had blasphemed the Lord. He did not forsake him). She ran to tell Peter and John because Mary, the Lord's mother, was living with John in his home. And with a woman's heart she wanted to let the Lord's mother know what was happening. You know if you look carefully at the scriptures you get these little personal things that bring out the character of various personalities of the scripture.) She told them that somebody had taken away the Lord.

Peter and John ran a race. Peter was an old fellow, Yes! He was getting old and he could not run as hard as he used to. John ran past him and got to the sepulchre first. But I will tell you something else, John was the tender shy disciple. He just stood there. But Peter was still the big bold blustering Peter. He did not wait at the door of the tomb, he ran right in to see what was happening. There are lessons there for us all!

I want to come now from the quest to the request.

TWO: THE REQUEST

You know Mary Magdalene is standing at the tomb weeping. The very thing she was weeping about she should have been rejoicing about. The empty tomb was not for tears but for triumph. How like the people of God. Many a time I have wept about things I should have rejoiced about. Perhaps it was a disappointment and I wept at the grave of disappointment. But I should have rejoiced. The thing the Lord withdrew from me and did not give me was for blessing and was not in order that I might weep.

Let us learn here, as believers, that the Lord does all things well. All He does He does with a hand of grace and a hand of love.

SITTING ANGELS

As she stands weeping at the tomb she looks in and she sees angels sitting. Angels do not usually sit, they usually stand. If you study the narratives you will find that the other women saw them standing. There are only three angels in the Bible who sat, and they were all at the resurrection. The angel rolled away the stone and he sat on the stone. He made the stone his pulpit. It is scriptural to have a stone pulpit! And there was an angel on a stone pulpit. That was a testimony to triumph.

When Mary Magdalene went in she saw two angels sitting. One at the feet and one at the head where Jesus had lain. You know, my friend, in between were the grave clothes, the sign of death. That is a fulfilment of a type. The first time angels are mentioned at the foot and at the head you find in Exodus 25:22. They were at the foot and at the head of the mercy seat. On the mercy seat there was the sign of death, the sprinkling of the atoning blood. God said, "Out of the midst of the mercy seat I will speak to you."

THE ANGELS' REQUEST

Now look at the angels' request in John chapter twenty and verse thirteen: "Woman, why weepest thou?" "What is the reason for your tears?" She turns and says, "Because they have taken away the Lord." No! "Because they have taken away my Lord." Oh, her heart is pent up with agony of frustration and disappointment and sorrow. She says "He is my Lord". David said, "The Lord is my Shepherd." In the Song of Solomon the Bride says "My Beloved is mine and I am His." Paul says, "He loved me and gave Himself for me." He is my Lord.

Mary was so taken up with the Lord that she had not any more time for the angels. How do I know? Because she turned herself back. She did not hold any more communion with the angels. She wanted her Lord.

THE LORD'S REQUEST

I want you to notice the Lord's request. He adds to the angels' request. He says, "Woman, why weepest thou? Whom seekest thou?" He knew that she was on a quest. "Whom do you seek Mary?" Notice carefully what is said. "She supposed Him to be the gardener." Many a time we supposed, when the Lord came to us, that He was someone else. We did not see His hand or hear His voice. When that great trial came to you, you did not think it was the Lord. You supposed it was the gardener, someone tending the plants and uprooting the weeds and doing the job of the garden. But it was the Master's hand that did it all. It was the Lord that did it! "She supposed Him to be the gardener."

She said an impossible thing, "Sir, if thou hast borne Him hence, tell me where thou hast laid Him, and I will take Him away." You know she never told who she was looking for. It does not say here that it was the Lord Jesus. She said "If thou hast born Him hence." There was only one Person uppermost in her mind and that Person was the Lord and she thought the gardener knew for whom she was looking. So she said "If thou hast born Him hence tell me where thou hast laid Him, and I will take Him away."

THIRDLY: THE BEQUEST

Look at His bequest. Jesus said unto her "Mary". When He calls His sheep He calls them by name, John 10:3: "And my sheep hear my voice and they follow me." He said "Mary," and she immediately recognised Him. "I have called thee by thy name, thou art mine."

My friend, is it not a wonderful thing when the Lord calls you by your name?

She replied "Rabboni". Rabboni is different from Rabbi. Rabbi means master. Rabboni means my Master. My Master!

There are three things. First of all there is a new relationship. She went as beforetimes to hold Him by the feet and worship Him. He says, "Touch me not." We are not to know the Lord Jesus any more after the flesh. We have entered into a new relationship. It is one of a divine and spiritual worship. It is no longer a fleshly worship. It is a spiritual worship! There is a new relationship here. "Mary," He says, "It is all changed, do not touch my feet, it is my presence spiritually that will bring you peace, not the physical touch of my resurrected flesh but the spiritual touch of my resurrection power."

There is a new relationship here. Look at it. "For I am not yet ascended to my Father: But go to my brethren." I want you to notice there is a new partnership. This is the first time that the Lord ever called His disciples "My brethren". In all the other parts of the gospel they were called "His disciples". But you know what it says? "After His death He is not ashamed to call them brethren." A new partnership! "He is the firstfruits." We are part now of a mystical union in the family of God because of His resurrection. So He says "They are my brethren."

And God the Father is your Father and He is my Father. He is your God and He is my God.

No wonder Thomas said "My Lord and my God." A new relationship! A new throneship! A new partnership! This is the bequest that is given to every child of God because of the resurrection.

Mary went back to tell but she was not believed, and you know we are telling the world of a resurrected Christ and they do not believe us. But, praise God, there is a remnant and Jesus said of those of us who believe: "Blessed are those that have not seen, and yet have believed." We did not see Him with the natural eye but we have seen the great truth of His resurrection with the eye of faith. May your eyes be opened to Behold Him.

Amen and Amen

4 The Fundamentalist *confession*

A SERMON PREACHED ON THE 32ND ANNIVERSARY OF HIS ORDINATION TO THE GOSPEL MINISTRY ON THE FIRST LORD'S DAY MORNING OF AUGUST, 1978 IN THE MARTYRS MEMORIAL CHURCH. THE TEXTS WERE LUKE 1:2 "THOSE THINGS MOST SURELY BELIEVED AMONGST US" AND LUKE 1:4 "THE CERTAINTY OF THOSE THINGS."

ON THIS 32nd ANNIVERSARY I wish to reaffirm my faith. I desire to make my confession. I want to declare where I have stood during my thirty-two years of ministry to the church and where I am going to stand, by God's grace, in whatever days are left to me.

My texts are Luke 1:2 , "Those things most surely believed amongst us" and Luke 1:4 says, "The certainty of those things."

It is not my purpose to enter into my particular adherence to what may be called a particular doctrinal or denominational interpretation. While I hold tenaciously to what has been commonly called the Reformed Faith, I am not prepared to unchurch all those who will not dot my "i"s or stroke my "t"s in theological interpretation. I intend to continue my ministry, as I have commenced it, and so far have maintained it, in majoring on those great fundamental truths of the Historic Christian Faith which have been declared and defended by Bible Christians of all denominations and all ages, or in other words, borrowing the inspired language of Luke, "Those things most surely believed amongst us."

I want to sum up "those things" under five heads.

I. I BELIEVE IN THE UNASSAILABLE BIBLE

The Bible is the Book of God and it is unassailable, that is proof against all attack. Of course it is always under attack but it remains impregnable. No potency can disintegrate this celestial granite.

The Bible is Unassailable in its Canon

The word, "canon" means primarily, a straight staff, and hence a measuring rod. The word comes to be used only of those books which were easily recognised, because of their internal evidence, as inspired by Almighty God and therefore part of the Divine Revelation. Counterfeit and apocryphal writings were labelled uncanonical.

I believe the 39 books of the Old Testament and the 27 of the New Testament to be the unassailable Canon of Holy Scripture.

There is not a book too many nor a book too few in the Sacred Volume. All are needed to make a perfect whole, and any addition would destroy the completed unity. Take the number of the Old Testament books, 39. If you add the three and nine together you get 12. That number will help you to remember that the Old Testament is all about the 12 tribes of Israel, yes and in the last book of the Old Testament, the book of Malachi, the priestly tribe has its final and honourable mention, "He shall purify the sons of **Levi**" Mal. 3:3. This, however, is closely followed with the expression "ALL Israel" Mal. 4:4, which includes the whole 12 tribes.

Note carefully that the last words of the Old Testament are a warning of a coming curse. How different are the last words of the New Testament. They are the promise of a coming Christ.

Now the number of the New Testament books is 27. Seven is the number of perfection and two reminds me of Him who is the Second Person of the Adorable Trinity. So when I think of the number of the books of the New Testament I think of the Perfect Revelation of our Lord and Saviour Jesus Christ. If I take the Old Testament number of books, 39, and multiply 3 by 9 I again get 27. For the New Testament is in the Old concealed as the Old Testament is in the New, revealed.

The Bible is unassailable in its **canon**.

The Bible is Unassailable in its Content

The Content of the Bible is the Christ. In the volume of the Book it is written of Him. The Scriptures simply pour forth the things concerning Himself. They speak of the King. Christ is the only way to the Father but the Bible is the only way to Christ. These are they which testify of Him.

The Saviour and the Scriptures bear a common yet uncommon name - The Word of God. The Infallible, Impregnable, Inerrant Word of God - ABSOLUTE - FAULTLESS - UNERRING - SUPREME!

The Bible is Unassailable in its Character

The Bible is a holy book, it is the Holy Bible. Those who read it are the best proof of that, for it makes men holy, leading them into and then on in the paths of righteousness. Its character is magnetic and dynamic. It both draws and empowers. Its uplifting, purifying and edifying influence is beyond dispute.

Will the Old Book stand, when the "higher critics" state
That grave errors are discovered on its page?
Will it save the sinful soul? Will it make the wounded whole?
Will its glorious truth abide from age to age?

Will its message still abide, when the scientists decide
That its record of Creation is untrue?
Tell us the ascent of man is by evolution's plan;
Will its principles the sinful heart renew?

When in language wondrous fair, "Christian Scientists" declare
That there is no evil, only mortal mind.
When mental treatment fails, and seeming death prevails,
May we in the Bible consolation find?

When infidels parade the mistakes which Moses made,
When the truth of Revelation they deny,
Will the Ten Commandments still the demands of justice fill?
Will its word support us when we come to die?

> *Yes, the Word of God shall stand, though assailed on every hand,*
> *Its foundations are eternally secure;*
> *It will bear the critic's test, and the idle scoffer's jest,*
> *Its saving truth forever shall endure.*

By God's grace I intend to continue to BELIEVE, PROCLAIM and DEFEND THIS UNASSAILABLE BIBLE.

II. I BELIEVE IN THE UNIQUE CHRIST

The Christ in whom I believe, is **unique in His Person.**

There is none like Him. He is the only Person who lived before He was born. I believe in His Preexistence. He was before all worlds. He is the Everlasting Son of the Everlasting Father. He is the Timeless Christ because He is the Eternal Christ.

His Birth was unique

He was born of a pure virgin. Man had no part in His begetting. The Holy Spirit originated and consummated the production of His body and human soul. He is the Almighty God enthroned in humanity.

His Ministry was unique

His Words and Works defy imitation and reproduction. They set Him apart. There is none like Him, no not one. None can match His Touch or Tongue.

His Bleeding is unique

In death He released Eternal Life for all ages. His blood-stream generated pardon for all the elect of God. His Cross is the Gateway to Heaven. It is really and truly the ladder to the stars, nay rather beyond the stars. His Passion threw across that great Divide between the thrice Holy God and sinful humanity an impregnable bridge of meeting supported by the twin pillars of justice satisfied and grace magnified.

His Burial was unique

The sacred interment of the impoverished Christ amongst the rich was the subject of prophetic anticipation.

His Bursting of the Tomb was unique

What world empire ever before strained all its powers to keep the dead in the tomb? What buried person just resurrected lingered at his own sepulchre to wipe away the tears of the sorrowing?

His Ascension was unique

Through it there came such power that cowards became champions and ignorant men wiser than the sages of all ages.

This is the Christ which we have preached and shall continue to preach. The Christ, Uniquely Born, Uniquely Ministering, Uniquely Bleeding, Uniquely Buried, Uniquely Bursting the Tomb, Uniquely Ascended and Uniquely Coming Again.

The Glorious Company of the Apostles Praise Thee.
The Goodly Fellowship of the Prophets Praise Thee.
The Noble Army of Martyrs Praise Thee.
The Holy Church throughout all the World Acknowledges Thee.
Thou Art the King of Glory, O Christ: Thou Art the Everlasting Son of the Father.

III. I BELIEVE IN THE UNCONGEALED BLOOD

We are informed that human blood can only be banked for some 14 days and after that it can no longer be used for transfusion purposes. Its power and usefulness is gone. Human blood perishes.

The Blood of Jesus, however, never loses its power.

I Believe in the Uncongealed Blood - It cannot lose Its Freshness

It is unaging and unchanging. It will not, it cannot perish. It is as fresh today as it was when it flowed from the opened veins of the Godman on the accursed tree.

Grace is flowing like a river,
Millions there have been supplied.
Still it flows as fresh as ever
From the Saviour's wounded side.
None need perish - all may live, for Christ has died.

I Believe in the Uncongealed Blood - It cannot lose Its Fulness

Everything necessary for the purpose of our sins and souls is in the Blood of the Lamb. Its value is immutable. Its purifying is eternal. The whole fulness of Christ's life on earth is in solution in the Blood of His Cross.

Here is a stream charged with such cleansing power and filled with such fulness divine that the sins of ages flee before it and the stains of millions disappear at its touch. Here is a washing so potent that it transforms the offspring of hell into the begotten of heaven and fits the once sinful soul for the companionship of God for evermore.

I Believe in the Uncongealed Blood - It cannot lose Its Flow

The Blood of the Sacrificial Lamb still flows for the cleansing of sinners. All the powers of hell in all ages have combined and contrived to dam back this mighty crimson tide of divine redemption but they have not and cannot succeed.

The flow is unstoppable. Omnipotence runs in this blood-stream and all opposition is swept way by its mighty torrent. Nothing can stand before it. It overcomes the devil in its onward upward sweep.

The Blood has its spring in heaven and to that Celestial habitation it will return, imparting heaven to all who wash in its cleansing wave.

Oh precious is the flow
That makes me white as snow
No other fount I know
Nothing but the Blood of Jesus.

I believe in the UNCONGEALED BLOOD OF THE LAMB.

IV. I BELIEVE IN THE UNPARALLELED GOSPEL

In the first chapter of Romans you will find three great titles of the gospel. In verse one it is **"the gospel of God,"** that underlines the **Source** and **Purpose** of the gospel.

The gospel is not man-devised but God-originated. Its source is Deity not humanity. Before it had its reception in man's heart it had its inception and conception in God's heart. The Purpose of the Gospel is God's purpose. Its aim is not the mere betterment of man but rather the glory of the Sovereign God.

In verse nine it is **"the gospel of His Son,"** that underlines the **Sacrifice** and **Passion** of the Gospel.

God, when He loved, loved as only God could, the whole world. It was Godlike to love the world. When God gave He gave as only God could give, His Only Begotten Son. It was Godlike to give His Son. We often emphasise the Cross Jesus bore as our Saviour but what of the Cross in the Father's Heart when He gave up His Son! It is the gospel of His Son.

What of that Passion of the Cross? He who was the Son learned obedience by the things which he suffered. What a lesson for the Son! What a lesson for angels! What a lesson for sinners! He who has not learned his letters in this crimson book can never, never know the gospel of His Son.

In verse 16 it is **"the gospel of Christ"** that underlines the **Salvation** and **Power** of the gospel.

The title Christ means "Anointed."

Christ is the Anointed Prophet of His People. The gospel is a Prophetic Word revealing to us the will of God for our Salvation.

Christ is the Anointed Priest of His People. The Gospel is a Priestly Word, it points to the Cross, to the Substitutionary Sacrifice for sin!

Christ is the Anointed King of His People. The Gospel is a Kingly Word, a sword, destroying all His and our enemies.

This is the Word that by the Gospel, the gospel of God, the gospel of His Son, the gospel of Christ, we preach unto you.

V. I BELIEVE IN THE UNLIMITED SALVATION

Men can be saved. Sinful men, vile men, rebellious men, can be eternally saved.

The salvation I believe in is **unlimited in its gospel offer**. The great commission says, "Go ye into all the world and preach the gospel to every creature." Mark 16:15.

Alas, the devil has so deceived professing evangelicals that they handle the text with as much unbelief as apostates handle deceitfully other verses of the Infallible Word.

In the name of their philosophy - I call it not theology - they seek to limit the field "all the world" to their own tiny denominational synagogue.

They go on to limit **the preaching**. It must not, they tell us, make a free offer of Christ. Such a free offer is against the logic of their scheme, their set of dogmas. To appeal to sinners to repent, as Paul did day and night with tears, is to them a human addition which is unnecessary. To press, in such a way, the claims of Jesus upon sinners is no part of their gospel preaching. "Compel them to come in," that text they have never in the deep agony of a passion for souls, considered, let alone practised.

They further limit **the people**.

God says "to every creature." They will offer Christ to the elect only. How they know the elect I have never yet learned.

Listen, "All that the Father giveth me shall come to Me, and him that cometh to Me I will in no wise cast out." John 6:37. If you come to Jesus it is proof positive that you have been given to Him by the Father, for v. 44 tells us that no man can come except the Father draws him. Oh come and welcome to Jesus.

Salvation is unlimited in its power. All who come unto God by Christ are saved to the very uttermost.

Salvation is unlimited in its enjoyment. It is eternal salvation. Its joys are inexhaustible and everlasting. O the happiness of the man whose sin is covered.

> *My soul, triumphant in the Lord,*
> *Shall tell its joys abroad;*
> *And march with holy vigour on,*
> *Supported by its God.*

> *Through all the winding maze of life,*
> *His hand hath been my guide;*
> *And in that long-experienced care,*
> *My heart shall still confide.*

> *His grace through all the desert flows,*
> *An unexhausted stream:*
> *That grace of Zion's sacred mount*
> *Shall be my endless theme.*
>
> *Beyond the choicest joys of earth*
> *These distant courts I love;*
> *But oh, I burn with strong desire*
> *To view Thy house above.*
>
> *Mingled with all the shining band,*
> *My soul would there adore;*
> *A pillar in Thy temple fix'd,*
> *To be removed no more.*

I want to close by quoting the words of a staunch Calvinistic Reformer, Samuel Rutherford the Covenanter, who said,

> *I have wrestled on towards heaven,*
> *'Gainst storm and wind and tide,*
> *Now, like a weary traveller*
> *That leaneth on his guide,*
> *Amid the shades of evening,*
> *While sinks life's lingering sand,*
> *I hail the glory dwelling*
> *In Emmanuel's Land.*

I want also to quote in contrast the words of a great Arminian preacher, John Wesley,

> *Happy if with my latest breath*
> *I may but speak Christ's Name,*
> *Preach Him in life*
> *And cry in death,*
> *Behold, behold the Lamb.*

Amen and Amen

5 The one and only subject *of the Gospel*

A SERMON PREACHED ON THE 45TH ANNIVERSARY OF HIS ORDINATION TO THE GOSPEL MINISTRY ON LORD'S DAY MORNING 4TH AUGUST, 1991 IN THE MARTYRS MEMORIAL CHURCH. THE TEXT WAS I CORINTHIANS 2:1 "FOR I DETERMINED NOT TO KNOW ANYTHING AMONG YOU SAVE JESUS CHRIST AND HIM CRUCIFIED."

ON THURSDAY 1st AUGUST, 1946 I was ordained to the Gospel Ministry in the old Ravenhill Evangelical Mission Church. Godly men, Rev. W. J. Grier, leader of the Evangelical Presbyterian Church, Rev. Thomas Rowan, Irish Presbyterian minister, Professor T. B. McFarlane, Reformed Presbyterian Church (in the Theological Hall of which Church I was trained for the Gospel Ministry), and my beloved father, Rev. J. Kyle Paisley, took part in the service.

On Lord's Day morning 4th August, 45 years ago I preached my first sermon as an ordained minister and shepherd of the flock over which the Lord had made me overseer.

The world famous evangelist Rev. W. P. Nicholson was in the congregation.

My text was I Corinthians 2:1:-

'*For I determined not to know anything among you save Jesus Christ and Him Crucified.*'

I wish to take that text again for my message on this 45th Anniversary Morning Service.

Notice five things in the text. They have all to do with the strategy of Paul's ministry.

Firstly, **How He Started** - *'I determined'*. He started with determination.

Secondly, **How He Was Situated** - notice the words *'Among you.'* Part of you; going in and out in association with you. The ministry is never ever a thing apart. It is something which involves the people and the preacher together.

Thirdly, **How He Was Schooled** - *'Not to know anything.'* What did he learn at school? He learned how not to know anything. Strange schooling! Not to know anything!

Fourthly, **How He Was Subjected** - *'Save Jesus Christ.'* Save Jesus Christ! He was a man of one subject, one theology, one doctrine, one Gospel, *'Jesus Christ.'*

Fifthly, **How He Stopped** - *'And Him Crucified.'* Where did he stop? He stopped at the Cross *'And Him Crucified.'*

FIRST - HOW HE STARTED

How he started, *'I am determined.'*

Paul was a determined man. This determination of Paul rested upon five pillars. It had a solid foundation.

Firstly it rested on the pillar that he was a **convicted** person.

If you turn to I Timothy you will find very briefly he gives his testimony. In verse 12 of chapter 1 of I Timothy he says, *'I thank Christ Jesus our Lord, Who hath enabled me, for that He counted me faithful putting me into the ministry, who was before a blasphemer, a persecutor and injurious.'*

This man Paul had a determination born out of conviction. He had discovered something that we had better all discover, that we are lost sinners and we need the Saviour. *'Who was before a blasphemer, who was before a persecutor.'* He sees himself standing there among the crowd holding the garments as they stoned Stephen- a persecutor and injurious, vexing the church of Jesus Christ.

Secondly, it rested upon the pillar that he was a **convinced** person.

He not only was convicted but he was convinced. Turn to the fifteenth chapter of the first epistle to the Corinthians verse eight and you will find that he talks there about what happened to him. He says, *'And last of all He* (that is Christ)*was seen of me also.'*

Oh yes as others had seen Him in the days of His flesh and had seen Him in His Resurrection Glory, so one day Paul saw the Saviour. He not only had a convicting work done within him, but he had a convincing work. He was totally and absolutely convinced of the actuality and reality of the Risen Son of God.

Thirdly it rested upon the pillar that he was a **converted** person.

Upon that road to Damascus, we read he said, *'Who art Thou Lord?'* 'The word came back, *'I am Jesus whom thou persecutest. It is hard for thee to kick against the pricks.'* Then Paul said, *'Lord, what wilt Thou have me to do?'* That is the question of a converted person. Upon the Damascus road Paul saw the light and the burden of his heart rolled away. He was soundly converted.

Fourthly it rested on the pilllar that he was a **commissioned** person.

If you turn to the ninth chapter of Acts and verse 15 you will find that the Lord said to Ananias, *'Go thy way, for he is a chosen vessel unto me to bear my name before the Gentiles and kings and children of Israel.'* Commissioned to carry the Name, *'To bear in his body the marks of the Lord Jesus.'*

Fifthly it rested on the pillar that he was a **consecrated** man.

He was consecrated. What does it say? Acts chapter nine and verse 20, *'And straightway he preached Christ in the synagogues that He is the Son of God.'*

Convicted, convinced, converted, commissioned, consecrated those are the five pillars which upheld Paul's impregnable determination.

You couldn't shake him. He was immovable. He was steadfast. He was unassailable. He had made up his mind that he was a man of one idea, of one subject. He could say, *'This one thing I do.'*

SECOND - HOW HE WAS SITUATED

Secondly, how he was situated - *'Among you.'*

Corinth was the commercial capital of Greece. Its strategic situation and position made it the Mecca of trade between East and West. Here the East and West did meet. It derived rich income through its narrow isthmus, a distance of less than five miles, joining the East to the West.

It was a city full of religion. It was a city of riches. It was a city of the righteousness of men.

Paul arrived there after the chastening of Athens where he was mocked by the Athenians - the Epicureans and Stoics of the capital city. He came knowing that there was going to be war in the city of Corinth.

The situation was most difficult. At the beginning he had just his two fellow tentmakers Aquilla and Priscilla with him and they themselves were exiles, expelled from Rome by the decree of Claudius Caesar.

As Paul walked around that great city he determined that come what may as long as God gave him strength and help, no matter how religious that city was, no matter how rich that city was, no matter how self-righteous that city was, he was going to stick to one thing and one thing only - Jesus Christ and Him Crucified.

He was going to strike at the falsehood of riches with Christ Who is the immeasurable riches of God. He was going to strike at the religion of Corinth with Christ Who is the sum total of all true religion and Who is Himself God's way, God's truth and God's life.

He was going to strike at all self-righteousness with Christ alone Who is made unto sinners in the Gospel Wisdom, Righteousness, Sanctification, and Redemption.

Yes, as he walked around Corinth he resolved, *'While I am with you in this city, while I sojourn amongst you, yes I will weep with those that weep. I will rejoice with those who rejoice. But through it all I am determined to proclaim Christ and Christ alone.'*

THIRD - HOW HE WAS SCHOOLED

Thirdly, how he was schooled - *'Not to know anything among you.'*
This was a determination to be a 'know nothing' - strange determination!
'But Paul, do you not know that this is a city of learning?'
'Yes, I know that, but as far as I am concerned I am going to be an illiterate. I know nothing.'
'But Paul, this is a city of wisdom.'
'Yes I know that, but as far as their wisdom is concerned I am a fool and I am going to remain a fool. I am determined to know nothing.'
'But Paul this is a city of riches.'
'Yes, I know that, but I am a pauper as far as the riches of Corinth are concerned, and I am going to remain a pauper.'
'But Paul, this is a city of eloquence.'
'Yes, I know that, but as far as the eloquence of Corinth is concerned I am a stammerer and I am going to remain a stammerer.'
'But Paul, this city is a city of religion.'
'Well, as far as I am concerned I am going to be the most irreligious person in the whole city, and at the end of my ministry I will still, by the religious standards of Corinth, be irreligious.
'But Paul, this is a city of progress.'
'Yes, I know that but as far as I am concerned I am going to be retarded and I am going to remain retarded.'

'But Paul, this is a city of castes.'
'Yes, I know that, but as far as I am concerned I am going to be an outcast from all the castes of this city.'
'But Paul, this is a city of glory.'
'Yes, but I am going to be a man covered with shame.'
Paul knew all about riches. Paul knew all about eloquence. Paul knew all about religion, progress, glory and learning.

Do you want to know what he thought of them? Turn to Philippians chapter 3 verse 4, *'But though I might also have confidence in the flesh. If any other man thinketh that he hath whereof he might trust in the flesh. I more: Circumcised the eighth day, of the stock of Israel, of the tribe of Benjamin, an Hebrew of the Hebrews; as touching the law, a Pharisee. Concerning zeal, persecuting the church; touching the righteousness which is in the law blameless. But what things were gain to me, those I counted loss for Christ, yes doubtless, and I count all things but loss for the excellency of the knowledge of Christ Jesus my Lord: for whom I have suffered the loss of all things, and do count them but dung, that I might win Christ.'*

That word *'dung'* does not occur anywhere else in the New Testament but here, it is not just ordinary dung. It is the dung that the dog has eaten and then vomited it out again.

All the learning and all the glory and all the progress and all the riches and all the wonder of Corinth and of the world he counted as dog vomit. That was how he counted it.

He was determined to know nothing.

FOURTH - HOW HE WAS SUBJECTED

How he was subjected, *'save Jesus Christ.'*

He was totally, absolutely, overwhelmingly, supernaturally subjected to Jesus Christ. He was the bondslave - in the Greek, the *'doulos'* - the *'property'* of the Son of God. He had no will but his Master's will. No service but his Master's service. No desire but his Master's desire. No outlook but his Master's outlook. He was Christ's prisoner. He was chained to Christ. Incarcerated with Christ. Pinned to the Son of God.

As in marriage *'these two are one flesh'* so in this mystical union between Paul and his Saviour he was one with the Son of God.

Yes after twenty-five years what does he cry, *'That I might know Him,'* 'But Paul, you have walked with Him for twenty-five years, you have talked with Him for twenty-five years, you have suffered with Him?' *'Yes, but I don't really know Him, because the depths of His Personality and Love are unfathomable and immeasurable. That I might know Him!'*

When one measures the paper and straw men of this 20th Century with this giant of the First, one sees why the church and its ministry is so impotent!

Here was consecration indeed. Christ was his all in all.

Here was concentration indeed. Christ was his only subject. Anyone else going into Corinth would talk about 'adopting a diplomatic course, proceeding along an educational pathway, to introduce Christianity by degrees, taking a step by step process.'

'No!' cried Paul, *'Christ is not diplomatic with error, He is intolerant to and with all error. There is no room for diplomacy here.'*

'Christ is not learned through education, Christ only becomes known by revelation. Therefore, as far as I am concerned, learning is taboo in this situation.'

When a true Gospel preacher preaches, people do not have any doubts about where he stands.

Number One - With Paul there was no doubt about the **Glorious Person of Jesus Christ.** No doubt about that!

Christ was no phantom to the apostle Paul. He was no ghost. He was a real genuine Man. He was bone of his bone and flesh of his flesh. He was Very Man of Very Man. He was born. He lived. He died. He rose again. He was praying in Heaven and He was coming again in all the power of His resurrection glory.

You listen to some preachers and you would not know what they believe about the Manhood of the Son of God.

We have a theory, a poisonous, heretical theory abroad among evangelicals that Christ could have sinned in the temptation. That is blasphemy! Christ was not tested in order to see could He sin. He was tempted in order to prove that He could not sin. Christ is not able to sin. The error is maintaining that 'Christ is able not to sin.' The truth is 'Christ is not able to sin.' That is the truth.

One Person With Two Natures! Paul believed not only in the Manhood of His Glorious Person but he also believed in the Godhead of His Glorious Person.

When you listened to Paul preaching you had no doubt that Jesus is God. If you listen to these modern preachers you do not know whether Jesus is really

God or not. They talk about 'His Divinity' and then they say 'All men are divine'. Christ is God. He always was God. He is God, He forever will continue to be God.

*Come all harmonious tongues,
Your noblest music bring,
'Tis Christ the everlasting God,
And Christ the man we sing.*

*No less Almighty at His birth,
Than on the throne supreme,
His shoulders held up Heaven and earth,
When Mary held up Him.*

*Without beginning or decline,
Object of faith and not of sense,
Eternal Ages saw Him shine,
He shines Eternal Ages hence.*

There is no doubt about it, Paul believed in the Glorious Person of Jesus Christ. Truly God and truly Man! *'I am determined to know nothing among you save Jesus Christ in His Glorious Person.'*

Number two - **The Gory Passion Of Jesus Christ**. There was no doubt with Paul about the Gory Passion of Jesus Christ. Ah, but this is what made the Jews and the Greeks in Corinth mad. *'Tell us not of that Roman act of death, tell us not of that barbaric tree. Talk not to us about resurrection. Babble no more about the cross.'*

But Paul cried, *'I am going to unveil the Gory Passion of the Son of God. I am going to preach about the Hill of Reproach. I am going to preach about a Place of Scandal and a Place of Shame. I am not going to stir one inch away from the burdened, blackened, battered, broken, bleeding Saviour. While it is repulsive to the senses of men, it pleased God to save men in one way only, by the shedding of Blood, for without the shedding of blood there is no remission of sin.'*

He preached Christ in His Glorious Person and he preached Christ in His Gory Passion.

Number three - **The Gospel Power of Jesus Christ**. There was no doubt with Paul about the Gospel Power of Jesus Christ. This Christ has real power, real life-giving power, saving power, converting power, transforming power, keeping power. Jesus saves to the uttermost all that come unto God by Him, seeing He ever liveth to make intercession for us.

What Gospel power Paul experienced in Corinth! The whole city, we were reading about today (Acts 18:1-17), was changed by that Gospel power.

Do you want to know the characters who were changed? Turn to I Corinthians chapter six. See there the sort of people who were changed by this Gospel power.

The sixth chapter verse nine says, *'Know ye not that the unrighteous shall not inherit the kingdom of God? Be not deceived: neither fornicators, nor idolaters, effeminate, abusers of themselves with mankind, thieves, covetous, drunkards, revilers, extortioners shall inherit the kingdom of God.'*

What a gallery of sinful rogues! Paul preached to this gallery of rogues - fornicators, idolaters, adulterers, effeminate, abusers of themselves with mankind, thieves, covetous, drunkards, revilers, extortioners and he says, *'Such were some of you, but ye are sanctified, but ye are justified in the name of the Lord Jesus and by the Spirit of our God.'* But ye are washed!

I know a Fount
Where sins are washed away,
I know a place where night is turned to day,
Burdens are lifted, blind eyes made to see,
There's a wonder working power
In the Blood of Calvary.

Gospel power!

Oh Lord, descend and fill this place,
With choicest tokens of Thy grace,
These walls we to Thy honour raise,
Long may they echo with Thy praise,
Here let the Great Redeemer reign,
With all the graces of His train,
While power Divine His Word attends,
To conquer foes and cheer His friends.

Jesus Christ in His Glorious Person.

Jesus Christ in His Gory Passion.
Jesus Christ in His Gospel Power.
That is the message and from that there can be absolutely no retreat.

FIFTH - HOW HE STOPPED

How he stopped! *'Him Crucified.'*
His task was to get sinners to the Cross. There he was able to leave them knowing full well that redemption ground is the sure door to resurrection glory.

It is my job, it is my task, it is my work as a preacher to get sinners to the Cross.

God has no further revelation to make to men but that old Cross. It is God's ultimatum. It is God's final. It is God's climax.

God can create ten thousand billion worlds, but He can never make another Cross. For the Cross is the ultimate of the energies of the Divine attributes united to carry out one great act - the act of redeeming sinners. Creation cost God His breath. Redemption cost God His Blood.

Creation could be destroyed by sin but the Cross can never be destroyed by sin, for the Cross has destroyed sin forever. *'For this purpose was the Son of God manifested, that He might destroy the works of the devil.'*

We live in a day when the so-called evangelicals want to escape the reproach of the Cross.

It used to be the Modernists (wrongly so-called because every modernist is an ancientist. There is nothing new about the devil's lie. It is as old as the devil himself), who denied the literal, actual, atoning Blood, the Precious Blood of Jesus. Now, however, in this apostate age we have the blasphemous denying work by so-called evangelicals.

Is it a literal Christ or a lost Christ that saves men? It is a literal Christ.

Is it an actual death or is it a philosophical decease that saves men? It is a literal death.

Is it actual Blood that alone can wash away sin or is it a figure of speech that washes away sin? It is actual Blood that washes away sin.

Do I understand it? No, I do not! Do I believe it? Yes, I do! Have I experienced it? Yes, I have. Hallelujah! I am determined to know nothing among you, save Jesus Christ and Him Crucified.

In so far as I have kept to the example of this great text in my forty five years of ministry God has put His seal upon it. In so far as I have departed from it, God's blessing has departed.

I want to repeat to you the words of Joseph Irons' immortal tribute to the Blood of the Lamb, for this is where we stop,

What sacred fountain yonder springs,
Up from the Throne of God,
And all new covenant blessings brings,
'Tis Jesus' Precious Blood.

What mighty sum paid all my debt,
When I a bondman stood!
And has my soul at freedom set,
'Tis Jesus' Precious Blood.

What stream is that which sweeps away
My sins just like a flood?
Nor lets one guilty blemish stay?
'Tis Jesus' Precious Blood.

What voice is that that speaks for me
In Heaven's High Court for good?
And from the curse has set me free,
'Tis Jesus Precious Blood.

What theme my soul shall best employ
Thy harp before Thy God,
And make all Heaven to ring with joy?
'Tis Jesus Precious Blood.

I spoke to a man the other day and he really opened his eyes. I said, 'You know I am a P.B. Preacher,' and he thought I had become a 'Plymouth Brother'. I turned to him and I said, 'No, PB stands for Precious Blood, I am a Precious Blood preacher.'

Sinner there is only one way to Heaven, it is by that Precious Blood that flows. Make sure you wash in it today. Wash and be clean!

If flows also dear backslider, to take away your backsliding. Wash in it and be restored today!

It flows also dear child of God, to renew your youth. Wash in it. For the Blood of Jesus Christ, God's Son, keeps on cleansing you from all sin.

And may we ever be determined to know nothing among you save Jesus Christ and Him Crucified!

Amen and Amen

6 Not ashamed *of the Gospel*

A SERMON PREACHED ON THE 45TH ANNIVERSARY OF HIS ORDINATION TO THE GOSPEL MINISTRY ON LORD'S DAY EVENING 4TH AUGUST, 1991 IN THE MARTYRS MEMORIAL CHURCH. THE TEXT WAS ROMANS 1:16 "FOR I AM NOT ASHAMED OF THE GOSPEL OF CHRIST."

ON THE 4th AUGUST, 1946, some forty-five years ago I commenced my ministry on this Road, and that evening I preached upon the sixteenth verse of the first chapter of Romans, *'For I am not ashamed of the Gospel of Christ.'* I want to take that text again after forty-five years of Gospel preaching and I want to preach again the very same Gospel which I preached when I commenced my ministry and which I have preached throughout these 45 years.

It is common today for a minister, when he remains for some considerable time in the ministry, to talk about the progress that he has made in his theology, in his philosophy, in his religious ideals and ideas.

Let me unashamedly confess that I have not made any progress whatsoever. I am preaching the very same Gospel which I preached on that occasion some forty-five years ago. I have not advanced to modern perceptions and philosophies concerning the Bible. I believe the Bible to be the Word of God. From the first *'In'* in Genesis to the last *'Amen'* in Revelation I believe it is God's Infallible, Inspired, Inerrant Word. I believe all that the Bible teaches. I do not profess to understand it all but I make public confession that I believe it all. Every word in this Book is the Word of God, and when the heavens and the earth pass away this Word shall never pass away.

At this time I do not want to prolong my remarks in that direction.

If you open your Bible at the first chapter of Romans and look with me at that chapter you will find that the Gospel is mentioned four times. Then if you look with me at the second chapter and at the verse 16 you will find it is mentioned again, *'In the day when God shall judge the secrets of men by Jesus Christ, according to my Gospel.' 'My Gospel'.*

I want to take the theme of the great apostle, *'I am not ashamed of the Gospel.'*

In Genesis you find a fallen man ashamed because of his sin. In Romans you find a fallen man, yet a redeemed man, not ashamed.

What makes the difference between Adam and Paul? Is it the Church? Is it the Sacraments? Is it Church Service? Is it Baptism? Is it Ritual Righteousness?

No! What makes the difference? It is the Gospel which makes the difference.

THE CAUSE OF THE GOSPEL

Now, in studying this repeated emphasis in these few verses of Paul on the Gospel we discover why he is not ashamed of the Gospel. Look at verse one of chapter one, he calls it the Gospel of God. There you have the cause of the Gospel: *'I am not ashamed of the cause of the Gospel.'*

Who caused the Gospel? What is its source? Where did it have its birth? What mind conceived it? What power begat it? What Being produced it? What might has maintained and sustained it?

Its cause is not found in a manward direction, its cause is found in a Godward direction. Its cause is not found in an earthward direction, its cause is found in a Heavenward direction. Its cause is not found in a Churchward direction, it is found, rather, in a Christward direction.

No man produced the Gospel. No Church produced the Gospel. No School conceived the Gospel. No Princes of this world begat the Gospel. It is not the manufacturing of man, it is the making of God. Paul emphasised that with all his heart.

Take your Bible and open it at I Corinthians 15:1-3.

What does Paul say?*'Moreover, brethren, I declare unto you the Gospel which I preached unto you, which also ye have received and wherein ye stand, by which also ye are saved if ye keep in memory what I preached unto you, unless*

ye have believed in vain. For I delivered unto you first of all that which also I received.'
Turn to the eleventh chapter of the same Book, I Corinthians 11:23. What does Paul say? *'For I have received of the Lord that which also I delivered unto you.'*
Turn to the great epistle of the Galatians chapter one and verse 12. What does Paul say? *'The Gospel which was preached of me is not* (mark it) *after man, for I neither received it of man, neither was I taught it but by the revelation of Jesus Christ.'*
'I am not ashamed of the cause of the Gospel.' It is the Gospel of God.

THE COST OF THE GOSPEL - THE GOSPEL OF HIS SON

Turn to Romans chapter one again. Look with me at verse nine and he calls it *'The Gospel of His Son.'*
There is the cost of the Gospel. I remember reading many years ago the three volumes of the life of Sir Edward Carson who became Lord Carson, the Founding Father of our Northern Ireland State.
In page 440 of the third Volume by Colvin we read of the great man's death bed. It records he had many visitors to his death chamber. One of them was the Primate of Armagh, Dr. D'Arcy. Carson said to him, *'Sir, I have seen much to shake my faith but what remains with me is no more than I learned at my mother's knee,* 'God so loved the world that He gave His only begotten Son, that whosoever believeth in Him should not perish but have everlasting life.' 'It is enough,'* the Primate said.
Lord Carson was right and so was the Primate, it is enough.*'God so loved the world that He gave.'* What did He give? His only begotten Son.
'I am not ashamed of the cause of the Gospel, it is the Gospel of God. I am not ashamed of the cost of the Gospel. The cost was the Son of God.' The Gospel of His Son!
What balances shall I bring? What scales shall I take? What measurements shall I call into play? What weight shall I employ to measure the cost of the Gospel?
The cost of the Gospel is threefold.
1. It cost the Father.
2. It cost the Son.
3. It cost the Holy Spirit.

What about the cost to The Father?

In giving His only begotten Son, in the giving of His beloved Son, in the giving of His Bosom Son, in the giving of His other Self.

What human mind can conceive the depth of this thought or attempt to scale its unscalable height, that God loved so much that He gave all that He could give? He gave His Son gladly to the curse of the Cross.

There is a verse in Isaiah 53 which staggers me every time I read that great chapter, *'It **pleased** the Lord to bruise Him.'*

The cost to the Father when the Son said, *'Farewell'* to Him in the ivory palaces of the Eternal Throne Room of the Shekinah Glory of the Everlasting Palace of the Eternal God.

He left His Father's Throne on High,
So free, so infinite His grace,
And bled for Adam's guilty race.

The cost to the Father!

What about the cost to the Son?

What did it mean, Lord Jesus, for Thou to leave the Father's Throne on High, and come to this sin-scarred, sin-cursed, sin-ruined world to be made sin for us, that we might be made the righteousness of God in Thee?

There are three things that we need to bear in mind if we would find out the cost to the Son. The cost of **His Birth**, the cost of **His Body**, and the cost of **His Bleeding**.

C. H. Spurgeon, the Prince of English Preachers, said, for an angel to become a worm would be humiliation indeed, but the Everlasting, Invisible, Pure Spirit God to take a Body, that is Humiliation that cannot be conceived or measured by human mind.

God the Son tied Himself forever to human flesh by the medium of the Virgin's womb, and He will remain and will always be from now and forever the Godman - the **Theanthropos** - the Man Christ Jesus. His Birth!

What about His Body? It was a prepared Body, prepared by the Holy Ghost in the womb of the Virgin, conceived by Deity that Deity might Incarnate Himself upon that which was conceived by Deity, for only that which is conceived by Deity can be indwelt by Deity. Oh, the wonder of it all! Oh, the cost! The Birth is to the taking of a Body and the Body was for the purpose of the Bleeding. When I go to Calvary and stand on the Hill of Reproach and see the Tree of Shame, hear the Godman cry in agony and see the Blood flow, every drop demands an answer to the question, *What is the cost of the Gospel?* It cost the Son His Life's Blood.

Oh, I know, today, that men do not want to hear this Gospel of Blood. An old Scotsman lay dying, his only daughter stood by her father's deathbed, and he took his hand in hers and said,

'There's nae Covenant noo lassie,
There's nae Covenant Blood.
There's nae altar noo lassie,
There's nae Lamb of God.
There's nae Spurgeon noo lassie,
There's nae guid McCheyne.
And the dear dear Cross they preached, lassie,
The dear, dear Cross is gone.
Folk dinny want the Cross, lassie
They've cuttin doon the Tree,
And naebody believes in it
But fules like you and me.'

And let me add **AND ME!** Let me add, for every child of God, **FOR ME TOO!** We believe in that old Cross. We believe in that Bloodstream that flowed from Emmanuel's veins. We believe in the Fountain filled with Blood. We believe it is the only way of Salvation.

On the golden streets of Heaven,
All men hope to walk someday,
But so many are not willing to accept the narrow way.
But while others build on good works
Or opinions if they may,
Hallelujah! I'm depending on the Blood!

What about the cost to the Holy Spirit?

God the Son entered a Body that was Sinless, but the Holy Ghost in order to redeem me enters a body that is full of sin.

He comes into this old corrupted, ruined, depraved, stained, sin-cursed tabernacle of the flesh in which dwelleth no good thing, and He takes the Precious Blood and works a work of mercy and salvation and redemption and a new birth.

What condescension that the Holy Spirit should deem to set His feet upon a ruined body like mine!

The little dove from Noah's Ark would not rest its feet on the waters of judgment but, thank God, the Blessed Holy Ghost has come into my sin-cursed heart and wrought salvation within my soul. The cost to the Holy Ghost!

I am not ashamed of the cost of the Gospel!

THE CONSTRAINT OF THE GOSPEL - PREACH THE GOSPEL

The third reference to the Gospel is in verse 15, what does it say? *'So as much as in me is I am ready to preach the Gospel to you that are in Rome also.'* Look at verse 14, *'I am a debtor both to the Greeks and to the Barbarians, both to the wise and to the unwise.'*

Here we have the constraint of the Gospel. *'I am a debtor,' 'I am ready to preach the Gospel,'* not *'A Gospel'* but *'The Gospel.'*

There is only one Gospel.

That Gospel is a paradox, it puts me out of my eternal debt to God, but puts me into everlasting debt to men. I am a debtor to preach the Gospel to every sinner in the world. I stand in debt, and I can only discharge that debt by telling men of the Saviour Who has saved my soul. I am a debtor to every sinner.

Sinners are catalogued in the Bible (Revelation 21:8). We read that sinners are **fearful**, I am a debtor to every fearful sinner to tell him of a Gospel that can take away his fears.

Sinners are **unbelieving**. I am a debtor to every unbelieving sinner to tell him that he can be saved and that faith is a gift of God, without money and without price.

I am a debtor to every **abominable** sinner because I must tell him that Christ saves to the very uttermost.

I am a debtor to every **murdering** sinner because a man that hates God is a murderer and yet God loves that man, and His grace alone can save the murderer.

I am a debtor to every **drunkard** sinner to tell him of the sweet wine, and if he drinks of the water of this wine he will never thirst again.

I am a debtor to every **gambling** sinner to tell him the folly of his ways, and to tell him of the One Who died within the sound of the dice of the gamblers at the rugged Tree called Calvary when they had their throw of the dice for His garments beneath the Cross.

I am a debtor to every idolatrous sinner, to every adulterous sinner, to every lying sinner, to every unclean sinner.

I am a debtor. I am ready to tell them of Jesus.

If you profess to have the experience of the Gospel and you do not feel the need to discharge your debt, if you cannot say tonight, *'I am ready,'* then, my friend, you have never experienced this Gospel. It sets us in the place of readiness to witness for Jesus Christ.

I am not ashamed of **the cause** of the Gospel.
I am not ashamed of **the cost** of the Gospel.
I am not ashamed of **the constraint** of the Gospel.

THE CONSEQUENCES OF THE GOSPEL - POWER UNTO SALVATION

Let us turn to verse 16, *'The Gospel of Christ.'* Here we have the consequences of the Gospel. What are the consequences of the Gospel? *'It is the power of God,'* there is the **strength** of the Gospel - *'unto salvation'*, there is the **salvation** of the Gospel - *'to everyone that believeth, to the Jew first and also to the Greek'*, there is the **scope** of the Gospel, the unlimited scope of the Gospel of Jesus Christ.

You stand before a heap of dynamite and you can argue that it is explosive material, but the way to prove it is to strike a match and set off the detonator and then you will prove it. One match is worth more than a ton of theory.

The Gospel displays to men in a demonstration of power that it is the very Gospel of Christ.

When our congregation had its pilgrimages we sojourned for a while in the Coalmen's Mission, that great nursery of revival down there on the Queen's Bridge. Then we pilgrimed for a while in the Ulster Hall while this Church building was being erected.

A prominent businessman in East Belfast attended the Ulster Hall every Sunday evening. He did not attend to listen to the message for the good of his soul. He attended because he was one of the best mimics in the entertainment world, and his greatest piece was mimicking *'my wife's husband'* as he preached.

Every Monday he would call his employees together, some 27 or 28 of them and he would go over almost word for word everything I had said in the Ulster Hall. Then he went out and did his star turns to the various great parties, his Masonic friends, his friends in Clubs and Pubs and dancehalls.

One night I preached in the Ulster Hall and he learned off that sermon. He went back to his home but the sermon that he had learned was being preached to him by the power of the Holy Ghost. The next morning his employees gathered and said, *'Were you at the Ulster Hall last night?'* He said, *'Yes.'*

'Are you going to do your turn?' they asked and he yelled out, *'No, get out.'* The employees fled from his presence. They asked, *'What is wrong with him?'*

That night in the old Manse on the Beersbridge Road the door bell rang and there he stood on the doorway. He burst into tears and said, *'Preacher, is there any hope for my soul?'* I brought him in. He told me the story and he said, *'It has been preached in my soul, preacher. There is a voice preaching your message and I can't escape from it, and I have no peace and I have no hope, I am lost.'*

I said, *'Friend, you may have no hope as you are, and you may have no peace but I know a place where there is peace and there is hope and there is pardon.'*

He was one of the scores of people who knelt at that old sofa in the drawing room of my home and sought and found the Saviour. I am looking at a young man sitting here tonight on my left-hand side and at that very sofa, he knelt and came to Jesus Christ.

When I was at the recent Constitutional Talks a civil servant approached me. He said, *'You do not know me, Mr. Paisley, or recognise me but my wife and I came to your home many many years ago and you led us to Christ and we found pardon through the grace of God.'*

A demonstration of the Gospel, the consequences, it is *'the power of God'* there is **strength**; *'unto salvation',* there is **salvation**; *'to them that believe, to the Jew first, and also to the Greek'* there is **scope**.

Man tonight, woman tonight, sinner tonight, boy or girl tonight without Christ, **you** can be saved by this Gospel.

THE CORONATION OF THE GOSPEL - MY GOSPEL

Finally, chapter two of Romans and verse 16. What a verse this is! What does it say? It says, *'In the day when God shall judge the secrets of men by Jesus Christ according to my Gospel.'*

The Gospel Ship has not had an easy voyage since it was launched by the Hand of Grace in the Red River of the Redeemer's Blood. Its passage has been stormy.

In 1809 a noted skeptic and infidel said, *'In a hundred years the only place you will find the Bible will be in a Museum.'* Following hard on his heels another infidel wrote an attack on Christianity *'which was going to bury Christianity forever'* and which he claimed was *'The Obituary of the Christian Religion'*. His name is forgotten but on the very site of the house where he wrote that particular attack there now stands a Gospel Preaching Church.

What am I talking about? I am talking about the Crowning, the Coronation of the Gospel. Through good report and ill report, through dark scandalous attacks and wicked frontal assaults this Gospel Boat will sail on and on until the great day shall arrive. That is the day which shall end all days and usher us from time to Eternity. Then when all days shall end the aeons of Eternity shall begin.

What does Paul say? *'On that day my Gospel will be crowned, for men will be judged according to my Gospel.'*

'But Paul, is it your Gospel?'

'Yes, it is my Gospel. I know it is God's but by my experience, by my committal and by the implantation of the Holy Spirit of God it is mine.'

It is my Gospel which is going to be crowned, and what a crowing that will be.

Many shall come from the east and from the west and shall sit down with Abraham, Isaac and Jacob in the Kingdom of Heaven (Matthew 8:11). All saved through this Gospel.

There are not half a dozen Gospels. There is only one Gospel. If any man preach any other Gospel unto you than that which we have preached, let him be accursed (Galations 1:8-9).

This is the only Gospel. I am not ashamed of it.

I am not ashamed of its **cause**.

I am not ashamed of its **constraint**.

I am not ashamed of its **cost**.
I am not ashamed of its **consequences**.
I am not ashamed of its **coronation**.

Have you believed it? Are you saved by it? Are you ready for the great day of God?

I have just one final thing to say to you, *'Believe on the Lord Jesus Christ and thou shalt be saved, and thy house!.'*

Amen and Amen

7 The Tears *of the Minister*

A SERMON PREACHED ON THE 47TH ANNIVERSARY OF HIS ORDINATION TO THE GOSPEL MINISTRY ON THE FIRST LORD'S DAY MORNING OF AUGUST, 1993 IN THE MARTYRS MEMORIAL CHURCH. THE TEXT WAS ACTS 20:19,31, 36-38 " SERVING THE LORD WITH ALL HUMILITY OF MIND, AND WITH MANY TEARS, AND TEMPTATIONS, WHICH BEFELL ME BY THE LYING IN WAIT OF THE JEWS. THEREFORE WATCH, AND REMEMBER, THAT BY THE SPACE OF THREE YEARS I CEASED NOT TO WARN EVERY ONE NIGHT AND DAY WITH TEARS. AND WHEN HE HAD THUS SPOKEN, HE KNEELED DOWN, AND PRAYED WITH THEM ALL. AND THEY ALL WEPT SORE, AND FELL UPON PAUL'S NECK, AND KISSED HIM. SORROWING MOST OF ALL FOR THE WORDS WHICH HE SPAKE, THAT THEY SHOULD SEE HIS FACE NO MORE. AND THEY ACCOMPANIED HIM UNTO THE SHIP."

WHEN I WAS ATTENDING the Theological Hall of the Reformed Presbyterian Church of Ireland (the Covenanters), a godly professor, Professor T. B. McFarlane, made all the students commit to memory Paul's great farewell charge to the elders of the church at Ephesus, where the apostle had been minister for three years.

That great apostolic charge is found in Acts chapter twenty verses seventeen to thirty-eight. I have never forgotten it and on the wings of memory it returns again and again to my mind.

In it Paul puts his whole Ephesian ministry under scrutiny and review. Before us we have the portrayal of the faithful minister of Jesus Christ which the immortal dreamer, John Bunyan, describes in his eternal dream, the Pilgrims

Progress, as that grave person with his back toward the world, his face toward heaven, the best of books in his hand and looking as if he pleaded with men.

In looking at this passage recently I was struck with the emphasis it makes on tears.

Verse 19: *'Serving the Lord with all humility of mind, and with many* **tears***, and* **temptations***, which befell me by the lying in wait of the Jews.'*

Verse 31: *'Therefore watch, and remember, that by the space of three years I ceased not to warn every one night and day with* **tears***.'*

Verses 36-38: *'And when he had thus spoken, he kneeled down, and prayed with them all. And they all* **wept sore***, and fell upon Paul's neck, and kissed him. Sorrowing most of all for the words which he spake, that they should see his face no more. And they accompanied him unto the ship.'*

The preacher who never weeps never really works. The preacher who never sobs never really supplicates. The preacher who never sheds tears really never shares triumph.

A tearless ministry is a dry, pathetic insult to both Deity and humanity. It is a travesty - the lie masquerading as the truth.

Now, Paul's great Exemplar and Example was our Lord Jesus Himself. The key to his ministry was his following hard in the footsteps of his Master. In verse 35 he calls for remembrance of our Lord Jesus Christ and his words:- *'I have shewed you all things, how that so labouring ye ought to support the weak, and to remember the words of the Lord Jesus, how He said, It is more blessed to give than to receive.'*

Notice, Paul had these words of our Lord by direct, divine revelation. Nowhere in the gospels are these words recorded nor is the incident narrated when they came from our Saviour's lips.

Now, tears are the common language of humanity which was not confounded at Babel. Bring a man from the snow of the Arctic and another from the sun of the Equator and if one commences to weep the other will get the message in humanity's common language of tears.

Mankind in every generation knows the meaning of tears.

That common language of humanity will end for the redeemed in heaven when God shall wipe it out forever. There we read of the redeemed, *'For the Lamb which is in the midst of the throne shall feed them, and shall lead them unto living fountains of waters: and God shall wipe away all tears from their eyes.'* Revelation 7:17 and also in Revelation 21:4, *'And God shall wipe away all tears from their eyes; and there shall be no more death, neither sorrow, nor crying, neither shall there be any more pain: for the former things are passed away.'*

In heaven the language of tears is forever a former thing.

That common language however will never end, for the reprobate in hell, forever there, shall be *'weeping and gnashing of teeth'* Matthew 8:12, 22:13, 24:51, 25:30, Luke 13:28.

SCRIPTURE REFERENCES TO TEARS

Tears

Now, the first reference to tears in our English Bible is 2 Kings 20:5 and Isaiah 38:5 (both these chapters of the Holy Scripture are one and the same). Here we have tears caused by pain of sickness and death. In these texts God 'sees the tears' of Hezekiah.

In the last reference to tears in the New Testament God sees the tears of the saints in order to wipe them away forever (Revelation 21:4).

The second reference in the Bible to tears is in Job 16:20. *'My friends scorn me but mine eye poureth out my tears unto God,'* thus confirming the Godward importance of human tears resulting from personal pain.

The thought that God sees tears, that tears are poured out unto God, and that God in the redeemed eternity will abolish tears, must not be forgotten in our study of this subject.

Weep

The first occurrence of the word 'weep' in Scripture is found in Genesis 23:2: *'And Sarah died in Kirjatharba; the same is Hebron in the land of Canaan: and Abraham came to mourn for Sarah, and to weep for her.'*

It is used of bereavement, of the parting of the ways at death, Abraham coming to weep in mourning over the death of his wife Sarah. The tears flowed at the pain of parting.

The second time the word occurs is in Genesis 43:30: *'And Joseph made haste; for his bowels did yearn upon his brother: and he sought where to weep: and he entered into his chamber, and wept there.'*

It is used of the pain of Joseph, still separated from his brother Benjamin.

The last time it is mentioned is in Revelation 18:11: *'And the merchants of the earth shall weep and mourn over her: for no man buyeth their merchandise any more.'*

The merchants, beholding the punishment of the great city of their merchandise and wealth, wept.

Weepest

This word occurs in our Bible in the form of a question to two women, one in the Old Testament and one in the New Testament, both were mourning for a son.

Hannah in the Old Testament in I Samuel 1:8: *'Then said Elkanah her husband to her, Hannah, why weepest thou? and why eatest thou not? and why is thy heart grieved? am not I better to thee than ten sons?'* Hannah was weeping for a son.

Mary Magdelene in the New Testament. The angels asked, *'Woman, why weepest thou? She saith unto them, because they have taken my Lord away, and I know not where they have laid him.'* John 20:13. The Lord asked her, *'Woman, why weepest thou? whom seekest thou?'* Mary was weeping for the Son of Man and the Son of God.

The mothers of Bethlehem wept at Christ's birth when their children were slaughtered by the cruel Herod. Matthew 2:18: *'In Rama was there a voice heard, lamentation, and weeping and great mourning, Rachel weeping for her children, and would not be comforted, because they were not.'*

The daughters of Jerusalem wept for the Lord Jesus as He went to the Cross. Luke 23: 28-31: *'But Jesus turning unto them said, Daughters of Jerusalem, weep not for me, but weep for yourselves, and for your children.*

For, behold, the days are coming, in the which they shall say, Blessed are the barren, and the wombs that never bare, and the paps which never gave suck. Then shall they begin to say to the mountains, Fall on us; and to the hills, cover us. For if they do these things in a green tree, what shall be done in the dry?'

Here were tears for judgment and punishment.

Note the source of weeping and tears:-

1. **PAIN**, bodily pain or otherwise.

2. **PARTING**, especially the parting of death.
3. **PUNISHMENT**.

TEARS IN THE LIFE OF CHRIST

Now, the Bible is one book. The greatest proof of its divinity is its indivisibility - its impregnable unity.

Three times we read of our Lord's tears. They fall into the same three categories:-

1. **PAIN** - in Gethsemane's garden, bodily pain and pain of mind and soul. Hebrews 5:7&8: *'Who in the days of his flesh, when he had offered up prayers and supplications with strong crying and tears unto him that was able to save him from death, and was heard in that he feared; Though he were a Son, yet learned he obedience by the things which he suffered.'* The awful pain in our Lord's body and human soul and human spirit not only pushed the blood through the pores of His body but the tears from His eyes. Hark to the strong crying and tears of the Godman on the ground in dark Gethsemane!

2. **PARTING** - the parting of death. John 11:32-36: *'Then when Mary was come where Jesus was, and saw him, she fell down at his feet saying unto him, Lord if thou hadst been here, my brother had not died.*

When Jesus therefore saw her weeping, and the Jews also weeping which came with her, he groaned in the spirit, and was troubled. And he said, Where have ye laid him? They said unto him, Lord come and see.

Jesus wept.

Then said the Jews, Behold how he loved him!'

3. **PUNISHMENT**. Luke 19:41-44: *'And when he was come near, he beheld the city, and wept over it,*

Saying, If thou hadst known, even thou, at least in this thy day, the things which belong unto thy peace! but now they are hid from thine eyes.

For the days shall come upon thee, that thine enemies shall cast a trench about thee and compass thee round, and keep thee on every side.

And shall lay thee even with the ground, and thy children within thee; and they shall not leave in thee one stone upon another; because thou knewest not the time of thy visitation.'

Note how this dovetails into the teaching of the rest of the Scriptures.

TEARS IN THE MINISTRY OF PAUL

Now notice the references in Acts 20 of Paul to a tearful ministry. Here is the very same divine order.

Acts 20:19: *'Serving the Lord with all humility of mind, and with many tears and temptations, which befell me by the laying in wait of the Jews.'* The PAIN, bodily pain.

Acts 20: 31: *'Therefore watch, and remember, that by the space of three years I ceased not to warn every one night and day with tears'*. The PUNISHMENT.

Acts 20: 36-38: *'And when he had thus spoken, he kneeled down, and prayed with them all.*

And they all wept sore, and fell upon Paul's neck and kissed him.

Sorrowing most of all for the words which he spake, that they should see his face no more. And they accompanied him unto the ship'. The PARTING.

TEARS, THE RESULT OF PAIN

Here was pain which came to Paul in the service of his Lord. Note the reference to the first day in Asia and all the seasons which followed. It was pain which started the tears from his eyes, not a few tears but many tears.

The days of service in Asia were days of cross-bearing. The road was hard and difficult.

When he arrived in Asia Minor from Cyprus his whole apostolic journeyings were beset with pangs, pains and persecutions, mainly originated by his own fellow-countrymen, the unbelieving Jews.

The wheel had turned completely. The Satanically-inspired, fast and fierce burning white heat of hatred which had motivated Paul himself to destroy the followers of the Lord Jesus, was now turned upon himself by those kindled by the same devilish flame.

Some of Paul's tears came because of deep, bitter remorse and regret of how he himself had murdered the innocent people of God. He saw in his persecutors and would-be murderers a mirror of himself in his unconverted days and what he saw he mourned with the mourning of true heart repentance. He saw again those innocent men, women and children to whose cries of mercy he had turned a deaf ear, and whom he had hounded to violent death, rejoicing over them as they were slaughtered. As he looked into the pit from which he had been digged and the rock from which he had been hewn, bitter tears from a broken and contrite heart flowed down his cheeks.

But tears were also his because of actual bodily sufferings. Paul wore a string of *perils* not *pearls*.

Comparing and contrasting himself with the other eminent members of the apostolic band he states: *"Are they ministers of Christ? (I speak as a fool) I am more; in labours more abundant, in stripes above measure, in prisons more frequent, in deaths oft. Of the Jews five times received I forty stripes save one. Thrice was I beaten with rods, once was I stoned, thrice I suffered shipwreck, a night and day I have been in the deep; In journeyings often, in perils of waters, in perils of robbers, in perils by the heathen, in perils in the city, in perils in the wilderness, in perils in the sea, in perils among false brethren; In weariness and painfulness, in watchings often, in hunger and thirst, in fastings often, in cold and nakedness. Beside those things that are without, that which cometh upon me daily, the care of all the churches. Who is weak, and I am not weak? who is offended, and I burn not? If I must needs glory, I will glory of the things which concern mine infirmities. The God and Father of our Lord Jesus Christ, which is blessed for evermore, knoweth that I lie not."* 2 Corinthians 11: 23-31

"Giving no offence in any thing, that the ministry be not blamed: But in all things approving ourselves as the ministers of God, in much patience, in afflictions, in necessities, in distresses. In stripes, in imprisonments, in tumults, in labours, in watchings, in fastings: By pureness, by knowledge, by longsuffering, by kindness, by the Holy Ghost, by love unfeigned, By the word of truth, by the power of God, by the armour of righteousness on the right hand and on the left. By honour and dishonour, by evil report and good report: as deceivers, and yet true; As unknown, and yet well known; as dying, and, behold, we live; as chastened, and not killed; As sorrowful, yet alway rejoicing; as poor, yet making many rich; as having nothing, and yet possessing all things." 2 Corinthians 6: 3-10

Ananias had a special message for Paul three days after his conversion. God said through him to Saul of Tarsus as he then was, *"For I will show him how great things he must suffer for my name's sake"* Acts 9: 16.

Those who serve Christ must suffer for him. Every one of the perils which he mentions conjures up in our mind the depths of bodily pain with which he was afflicted. No wonder the tears flowed.

Note the climax of those perils. Verse 26 of 2 Corinthians, chapter eleven: *"In peril amongst false brethren"*. Here is the cruellest cut of all.

The great Caesar's last words were made immortal by Shakespeare. When his bosom friend Brutus struck the final blow Caesar cried, *"Thou too Brutus!"*

No tears are so salted and bitter as the tears shed over the traitor.

David's tears over the treachery of Absalom! How dark and fearsome they were! *"Would God I had died for thee!"* 2 Samuel 18: 33

"Demas hath forsaken me," Paul cries, *"having loved this present world."* 2 Timothy 4: 10.

"All they which are in Asia be turned away from me." 2 Timothy 1: 15 - Paul's torment was bitter over the treachery of all those churches in Asia he had founded.

Every man of God has walked this way and has had to lament with David, *"Yea mine own familiar friend in whom I trusted who did eat of my bread hath lifted up his heel against me."* Psalm 41: 9

I can testify that in the many battles and conflicts in which I have been engaged during my 47 years of ministry in this city, the blows which struck the hardest and the wounds that went the deepest were struck by the hands of one-time loyal friends.

The Judas blow is the hardest. The Iscariot's cut is the most cruel. Nothing can bring forth tears of anguish like these wounds.

During my ministry I have felt the traitor's knife in my back on numerous occasions. Those experiences have been the most bitter and heart rending.

The traitor's kiss and the traitor's knife are instruments of the most deadly kind, drawing forth the very life's blood of the soul.

Severe pain, bringing tears, also comes from God's providential dealings with His ministers. The thorn of the flesh is the common lot of His servants.

Paul had this to say: *"And lest I should be exalted above measure through the abundance of the revelations, there was given to me a thorn in the flesh, the messenger of Satan to buffet me, lest I should be exalted above measure. For this thing I besought the Lord thrice, that it might depart from me. And he said unto me, My grace is sufficient for thee: for my strength is made perfect in weakness. Most gladly therefore will I rather glory in my infirmities, that the power of Christ may rest upon me. Therefore I take pleasure in infirmities, in reproaches, in necessities, in persecutions, in distresses for Christ's sake: for when I am weak, then I am strong."* 2 Corinthians 12: 7-10.

TEARS, THE RESULT OF PUNISHMENT

The minister of God has a solemn warning ministry - that ministry can be effective only if it is bedewed with tears. Dry, hard words of warning lead to letter preaching and the letter killeth - it is the Spirit who quickeneth and giveth life.

Paul declared, *"Knowing therefore the terror of the Lord, we persuade men; but we are made manifest unto God; and I trust also made manifest in your consciences."* 2 Corinthians 5: 11.

The terror of the severity of the Lord draws out the tears of the servant of the Lord.

The tears of the minister come as a result of his vision of the lost souls of men and their partaking of God's awful and eternal wrath.

Jeremiah's weepings and tears illustrate and underscore this.

"Oh that my head were waters, and mine eyes a fountain of tears, that I might weep day and night for the slain of the daughter of my people! Oh that I had in the wilderness a lodging place of wayfaring men; that I might leave my people, and go from them! for they be all adulterers, an assembly of treacherous men. And they bend their tongues like their bow for lies: but they are not valiant for the truth upon the earth; for they proceed from evil to evil, and they know not me, saith the Lord." Jeremiah 9: 1-3.

Nothing can melt the heart of hard sinners like the tears of the preacher.

Unless the preacher cries to God for mercy for his hearers, his hearers will not cry to God for mercy for themselves. Unless the preacher weeps for the salvation of souls, souls will not weep for their own salvation. Unless the preacher sheds his sobs his people will not shed their sins.

The one outstanding thing which the aged Paul remembered about the ministry of young Timothy was his tears. He desired to see him again and he says:

"Greatly desiring to see thee, being mindful of thy tears, that I may be filled with joy;" 2 Timothy 1: 4.

He marks in the next verse that these tears come from the "unfeigned faith" that was in him. The cross reference to that text is 1 Timothy 1: 5 *"Now the word of the commandment is love out of a pure heart, and of a good conscience and of faith unfeigned."*

Here is the source of tears, 1, unfeigned faith; 2, a good conscience; 3, a pure heart and 4, love. Feigned means a mere show, an exercise in hypocrisy - an act of dissimulation. *"Let love be **without dissimulation**. Abhor that which is evil; cleave to that which is good."* Romans 12: 9.

The word occurs six times in the New Testament. The other references are:

2 Corinthians 6: 6: "*Giving no offence in any thing, that the ministry be not blamed: But in all things approving ourselves as the ministers of God, in much patience, in afflictions, in necessities, in distresses. In stripes, in imprisonments, in tumults, in labours, in watchings, in fastings: By pureness, by knowledge, by longsuffering, by kindness, by the Holy Ghost, by **love unfeigned**, By the word of truth, by the power of God, by the armour of righteousness on the right hand and on the left. By honour and dishonour, by evil report and good report: as deceivers, and yet true; As unknown, and yet well known; as dying, and, behold, we live; as chastened, and not killed; As sorrowful, yet always rejoicing; as poor, yet making many rich; as having nothing, and yet possessing all things. O ye Corinthians, our mouth is open unto you, our heart is enlarged. Ye are not straitened in us, but ye are straitened in your own bowels.*" 2 Corinthians 6: 3-12. It is also mentioned in 1 Peter 1: 22 connected with "unfeigned love". In James 3: 17 it is translated "without hypocrisy".

Oh for a baptism of such tears. Paul shed these tears day and night. Tears were his constant diet. No wonder his vision was so clear. His tears washed all the dust of the old polluted world from his eyes and enabled him to see afar off. He was the long-sighted Paul.

This was the secret of McCheyne's ministry - his tears of love broke the hearts of the people.

Note carefully that the tears of Paul were shed as he viewed the punishment of God on the apostasy of his generation.

There can be no real love for the flock of Christ if the preacher refuses to fight the wolves which destroy the flock. Today, supposedly good men are strangely silent and unconcerned about the satanic attacks launched against the Lord Jesus Christ and his body on earth.

They have a feigned love and a feigned faith when it comes to the harsh realities of the apostasy of Christendom today.

Their silence gives consent. Their fellowship with the hirelings of Antichrist is an act of treachery to the true Christ whom they profess to serve. Their failure to protest when the most awful denials of the faith and the most outrageous blasphemies are uttered against the Saviour places them in the ranks of the enemies of the Gospel.

Note carefully the origin of the tears of Paul in this particular passage: *"For I know this, that after my departing shall grievous wolves enter in among you, not sparing the flock. Also of your own selves shall men arise, speaking perverse things, to draw away disciples after them. Therefore watch, and remember, that by the space of three years I ceased not to warn every one night and day with tears."* Acts 20: 29-31.

Here we have the two pronged attack on the Church - the outside attack and the inside attack.

THE OUTSIDE ATTACK

The outside attack, grievous wolves entering in not sparing the flock. Paul is echoing the words of the Saviour Himself in the Sermon on the Mount.

"Beware of false prophets, which come to you in sheep's clothing, but inwardly they are ravening wolves. Ye shall know them by their fruits. Do men gather grapes of thorns, or figs of thistles? Even so every good tree bringing forth good fruit; but a corrupt tree bringeth forth evil fruit. A good tree cannot bring forth evil fruit, neither can a corrupt tree bring forth good fruit. Every tree that bringeth not forth good fruit is hewn down, and cast into the fire. Wherefore by their fruits ye shall know them. Not every one that saith unto me, Lord, Lord, shall enter into the kingdom of heaven; but he that doeth the will of my Father which is in heaven. Many will say to me in that day, Lord, Lord, have we not prophesied in thy name? and in thy name have cast out devils? and in thy name done many wonderful works? And then will I profess unto them, I never knew you: depart from me, ye that work iniquity." Matthew 7: 15-23.

The grievous wolves disguised in sheep's clothing are pillaging the church today.

The recent annual conference of the Methodist Church passed a resolution celebrating the ministry of gays and lesbians in the church . Imagine the Church which was founded to spread holiness in the land, embracing the dunghills of Sodom.

"They that did feed delicately are desolate in the streets: they that were brought up in scarlet, embrace dunghills." Lamentations 4: 5

That's the scarlet sin alright!

"Also of your own selves shall men arise, speaking perverse things, to draw away disciples after them." Acts 20: 30.

Perverse doctrines and practices will come forth from the heart of the church itself. The very elders of the church will sell themselves out for personal advantage, and divide the church in factions for the sole purpose of making disciples for themselves.

How the history of the church illustrates this over and over again. Amidst his constant weeping the apostle issued solemn warnings about what the future held. This sad state resulted from a departure from their first love.

"Unto the angel of the church of Ephesus write: These things saith he that holdeth the seven stars in his right hand, who walketh in the midst of the seven golden candlesticks:" Revelation 2: 1.

"Nevertheless I have somewhat against thee, because thou hast left thy first love." Revelations 2: 4

"Remember therefore from whence thou art fallen, and repent, and do the first works; or else I will come unto thee quickly, and will remove thy candlestick out of his place, except thou repent." Revelation 2: 5.

Alas, the Church did not repent and the candlestick was removed. No wonder Paul wept day and night with tears.

There is another passage of scripture which parallels this one.

"Brethren, be followers together of me, and mark them which walk so as ye have us for an ensample. (For many walk, of whom I have told you often, and now tell you even weeping, that they are the enemies of the cross of Christ: Whose end is destruction, whose God is their belly, and whose glory is in their shame, who mind earthly things]." Philippians 3: 17-19.

TEARS, THE RESULT OF PARTING

"And when he had thus spoken, he kneeled down, and prayed with them all. And they all wept sore, and fell on Paul's neck, and kissed him. Sorrowing most of all for the words which he spake, that they should see his face no more. And they accompanied him unto the ship." Acts 20: 36-38.

Note the verses 25-27: *"And now, behold, I know that ye all, among whom I have gone preaching the kingdom of God, shall see my face no more. Wherefore I take you to record this day, that I am pure from the blood of all men. For I have not shunned to declare unto you all the counsel of God."*

Paul's time to go had come. The day of parting arrives for us all. The family breaks up and so does the church family.

Old Father Time with the scythe of death works in every church field. Ah, what tears we have shed as we have seen Christian brothers and sisters taken away from us.

Good men and good women - some have lived on borrowed time and long outrun the threescore years and ten. Others barely reached that allocated time span. Some were plucked away in full bloom of youth. Some fell to the reaper with the dew of childhood undried upon their brows. Ah, there were many tears at the parting.

All the members of my first and second Kirk Sessions under whom I served are gone, save one member. Our brother John Compton, hale and hearty, is still with us. Long may he be spared. There are but two members surviving who joined to give me the call to my life's work upon this road.

The tears are ours.

God has long since wiped from the eyes of the glorified saints all tears. We are left in the sunset. They are in the sunrise.

Some day another will minister at this desk and lead this flock. This under shepherd will have been ordered by the Great Shepherd of the sheep to leave down his rod and staff and enter future service where, praise God, sin can never sully and failure can never be known.

There were tears for Paul at the fork in the road that day by the seashore. Some of those who kissed him became those who led the church against him. Before his martyrdom the great apostle recorded that all Asia including Ephesus had turned against him. No wonder Paul's tears were bitter that day.

CONCLUSION

I would conclude this sermon with the words of a hymn which my Father had engraved on his tombstone. I often heard him quote them from the pulpit:-

Midst the darkness, storm, and sorrow,
One bright gleam I see;
Well I know the blessed morrow
Christ will come for me.
Midst the light, and peace, and glory
Of the Father's home,
Christ for me is watching, waiting,
Waiting till I come.

Who is this who comes to meet me
On the desert way,
As the Morning Star foretelling
God's unclouded day?
He it is who came to win me
On the cross of shame;
In His glory well I know Him,
Evermore the same.

Oh! the blessed joy of meeting,
All the desert past!
Oh! the wondrous words of greeting
He shall speak at last!
He and I, together entering
Those bright courts above;
He and I, together sharing
All the Father's love.

He, who in His hour of sorrow
Bore the curse alone;
I, who through the lonely desert
Trod where He had gone.
He and I in that bright glory
One deep joy shall share:
Mine, to be for ever with Him,
His, that I am there.

"And God shall wipe away all tears from their eyes; and there shall be no more death, neither sorrow, nor crying, neither shall there be any more pain: for the former things are passed away. Revelations 21: 4.

Amen and Amen

8 The Temptations *of the Minister*

A SERMON PREACHED ON THE 47TH ANNIVERSARY OF HIS ORDINATION TO THE GOSPEL MINISTRY ON THE FIRST LORD'S DAY EVENING OF AUGUST, 1993 IN THE MARTYRS MEMORIAL CHURCH. THE TEXT WAS II CORINTHIANS 5:13 "FOR WHETHER WE BE BESIDE OURSELVES IT IS TO GOD, OR WHETHER WE BE SOBER, IT IS FOR YOUR CAUSE."

THERE IS NO WORK which makes a greater demand upon the human being than the work of the Christian ministry.

No wonder Paul cried out, 'Who is sufficient for these things?' Not one. Our sufficiency is from God alone.

The minister is a man subject to like passions as other men, yet called to be a person through whom God doth beseech men to be reconciled to Himself.

II Corinthians 5:20: *'Now then we are ambassadors for Christ, as though God did beseech you by us: we pray you in Christ's stead, be ye reconciled to God.'*

The world's response to the man who claims to be an Ambassador for Christ is set out in Paul's proposition in verse 13 of II Corinthians 5:- 'For whether we be beside ourselves it is to God'. The world thinks such a man is mad.

Perhaps I should here define the term 'temptation'. There is a difference between trial or testing and temptation which is an allurement to sin. Where the word 'tempt' is used of God it means testing.

I am dealing not with the testing or trial of the minister but with the temptation of the minister, the ploy of the world, the flesh and the devil, to allure the minister to sin.

The minister is a much tempted man. The leader is more important than the led. Down the leader and only a mopping-up operation is necessary. Now there are temptations which are common to all men.

In every walk of life men are tempted through women, alcohol, money and pride. How many men, prominent men, able men, clever men, talented men, have bitten the dust through one or more of these temptations. Ministers have also fallen by temptations through these particular snares.

But there are special temptations to which the minister of Christ is prone and it is to these that I want to address your attention tonight.

There are temptations to which ministers fall a prey but they continue to pursue their ministries without any real attention being paid to them. They are not disgraced. They are not exposed. They are not condemned. In fact many of them are still reckoned to be successful in their ministries.

Yet through falling by these temptations their ministries are destroyed. Their labours are devalued. Their harvests are total barrenness. Their service is reprobate.

Remember Paul's determination: 'But I keep under my body and bring it into subjection; lest that by any means when I have preached to others I myself should be a castaway.' I Corinthians 9:27.

Cast from the hand of God because I am no more useable or useful in God's service!

The minister can remain in his pulpit and pastorate for years after he has been cast away from any further usefulness.

His preaching might continue to be fundamental, orthodox, scripturally sound, but as far as usefulness is concerned it is only a sounding brass or a tinkling cymbal (I Corinthians 13:1). His soul may be saved and if he is a soundly converted man he will be saved so as by fire, but his service is damned. It only awaits the judgment fire to destroy the wood, the hay and the stubble that it is. As an unfaithful watchman he will suffer loss, and what a loss, in the day of the judgment.

How many young preachers set out with great hope, great courage, great joy and great fire. But soon their hopes are dashed, somewhere down the line their courage evaporates, somehow their joys are lost and the fire which gave such promise becomes a heap of ashes.

What happened? It was not some of the coarser sins of the flesh which scissored off their locks of strength. It was not by women or wine or money or pride they fell. No, but it was by temptations specially hatched for ministers by Satan which brought about their downfall.

Jehu asked as he saw the heads of the sons of Ahab piled at the gate of Samaria, 'Who slew all these?' (II Kings 10:9). We might well ask the same question as we see the skulls of preachers of great promise which litter the church today, Who slew all these?

Let me list some of the temptations which have brought about the downfall of useful ministers and which constantly beset every minister of Jesus Christ.

THE FIRST TEMPTATION - HUMAN PRACTICE VERSUS THE DIVINE PRIORITY

The Divine Priority has been set for us and by public profession every minister has witnessed his total and unreserved commitment to it. Here it is - loud, clear and irrefutable, from the lips of the Saviour.

'But seek ye first the kingdom of God, and his righteousness; and all these things shall be added unto you.

Take therefore no thought for the morrow: for the morrow shall take thought for the things of itself. Sufficient unto the day is the evil thereof.' Matthew 6:33-34.

But the world, the flesh and the devil, all put up against adherence to that priority - they demand conformity to the usual human practice where the kingdom of man takes first place, smug self-righteousness second place, thoughts of tomorrow third place.

'Set your affections on things above,' that's the Divine Priority. Human practice cries out, 'Mind the things below.'

'Be not conformed to this world,' that's the Divine Priority. Human practice demands, 'Conform, conform.'

The minister is called to go against the stream. He must swim against the tide. He must not dare, nor think, nor consider conformity. He has but one priority - the kingdom of God. His citizenship is in heaven. He has an ambassadorship from heaven. He's in the world on business for another world. To become naturalised to this world is to become a traitor to the world above. His marching orders are from there and to there he is going. He cannot and must not change direction. The whole world below will pressurise him but he must not heed them. His congregation may want him to give a little but give he will not. His priority is fixed like the pole star. To deviate one iota is the beginning of the end. The smallest hole can sink the greatest ship. What a great fire a little flame can ignite. What a calamity a little poison can accomplish.

No, I must not deviate. I must get my priorities right. I must not exchange them for human practices.

THE SECOND TEMPTATION - PROFESSIONALISM VERSUS PROFESSION

The ministry is a profession but must never be professional. The minister has a profession to make, as Christ witnessed a good confession before Pontius Pilate (I Timothy 6:12).

Paul commends young Timothy upon his profession and says that he witnessed a good profession before many witnesses. (I Timothy 6:13).

How easily professionalism erodes that good profession. The minister becomes an actor, or a mere performer. His talk deteriorates into mere cant. His is a vain show in the flesh.

There is no kernel, only husks, pig's food - the husks which the swine did eat.

The pulpit is debased to a stage, the minister simply says his lines. Everything is unreal. Reality is missing. The outward has suffocated the inward and the Godward. The whole is meaningless - a religious sham and ecclesiastical deceit.

The minister becomes a professional performer. He reads the Bible not for his soul but for his sermon. He prays, not for power but for self-confidence. He does his duties as a mere routine. It is all spiritually lifeless. Oh it may have dignity but it is the dignity of the corpse. It may have decorum, but it is the decorum of the coffin.

The hand of professionalism paralyses the preacher. His zeal grows dull. His soul becomes lean. His sermons betray his declension.

He may shake himself like Samson but his power is gone and soon will the uncircumcised make him the object of their sport.

True profession leads, as it did for Christ, to the Cross. A Crossless preacher can never be a true minister of Jesus Christ. Professionalism will stifle true profession. The people will soon recognise the nakedness of his soul and the barrenness of his labours. His decline will be reflected on his church. No minister lives to himself. He is in the highest sense, his brother's keeper.

I have a profession to make on the claims of God to your soul. I must burn with earnestness and be consumed with zeal. Such zeal will break the strait-jacket of professionalism and breathe the reality of eternity into my pulpit work.

I must live every hour in the dazzling sight of the great immensities and the endless eternities. The immeasurable holy truths of the Holy Book must be my constant meditation.

I traffic for souls. I merchandise with the gems of eternity. I must never lose the awe of the heights of God.

A great Victorian preacher asked, 'Will a man leave the snow of Lebanon?' The tragedy is we do, and alas don't even know we do.

THE THIRD TEMPTATION - PRAYERS VERSUS PRAYING

It is in the closet the minister is made. It is outside the closet he is unmade. Hugh Price Hughes exclaimed one day, 'The evangelical preacher is always on the brink of the abyss.' The brink between prayers and praying is an abyss indeed.

Prayers are things of speech, praying is a thing of the soul.

When a minister leaves off praying and starts saying prayers then the day of calamity for him has come.

Prayers are cheap. Praying is costly.

Look at Christ. In the days of His flesh He offered prayers with strong crying and tears. Costly? And being in agony he prayed more earnestly and sweat as it were great drops of blood falling down to the ground. Costly? What price? The life's blood itself.

The praying minister is a man of power. He has the power that excells and only he possesses it.

To be leagued with Christ in the ministry of intercession is the harness of power. To know nothing of that holy yoke is to know nothing of that holy power.

The minister who runs in that partnership will never speak to man until he has first spoken to God. He will not do anything with his hands until he has been on his knees. His eye will light on God's Word first before lighting on other papers and letters.

The minister who has yielded to saying prayers rather than praying is working 'from beneath' rather than 'from above'.

THE FOURTH TEMPTATION - PARTY VERSUS PRINCIPLES

There is a generation which draws away the minister from principles and makes him a mere party man.

The party men are like the nine lepers who had faith and nothing else.

The principled man is like the one leper who returned to give Jesus thanks. He had gratitude as well as faith.

The minister who doesn't lose his gratitude to Jesus will not lose his principles either. It is the heart of thankfulness which throbs with loyalty and fidelity. It beats true.

If I really love my Lord I'll not sell His principles. If I don't really love Him I'll not be too much in love with His principles either.

What shall I care for party when principles are at stake? Let the party perish, let my Lord be exalted. Let my name be kicked in the gutter, let His Holy Name excel for ever.

Every enemy of my Lord is my enemy. I will not compromise His Truth nor allow His Person and Passion to be vilified. I must, I will, I can, I shall, Stand up for Jesus.

Cost is not to be considered. Christ is everything.

No words of mine could be too strong to condemn those who blaspheme my Lord and destroy His Character and Cross. They are of the brood of Judas, the offspring of the Iscariot, the generation of the viper, Satan, the vomit of hell itself.

I will not join with them in any spiritual relationship. I spurn the unequal yoke. I will not be harnessed with Belial or be in tandem with the devil.

Those who choose the unequal yoke are mere party men, unprincipled, ecclesiastical vagabonds, unworthy of their profession.

It was Dr. Jowett who said:

'I suppose that one of the deepest characteristics of worldliness is an illicit spirit of compromise. It calls itself by many agreeable names such as 'expediency,' 'tactfulness,' 'diplomacy,' and it sometimes ascends to high rank and claims kinship with 'geniality,' 'sociability,' and 'friendship'. But, despite this fine borrowed attire, the worldly spirit of compromise is just the sacrifice of the moral ideal to the popular standard, and the subjection of personal conviction to current opinion. There is a half cynical counsel exposed in the book of Ecclesiastes which exactly describes what I am seeking to express. 'Be not righteous overmuch ... Be not overmuch wicked.' I think this moral advice enshrines the very genius of worldliness. Worldly compromise takes the medium-line between white and black, and wears an ambiguous grey. It is a partisan of neither midnight nor noon. It prefers the twilight, which is just a mixture of midnight and noon and is equally related to both. It is, therefore, a very specious presence, fraternising with all sorts and conditions of men, nodding acquaintedly to the saint, and intimately recognising the sinner, at home everywhere, mixing with the worshippers in the temple, or with the money-changers in the temple courts. Grey is a very useful colour; it is in keeping with a wedding or a funeral, And yet the word of Holy Writ is clear and decisive, raising the most exalted standard: 'Keep thy garments always white."

Oh how pathetic is that minister who, with the overcoming of Divine Priorities by Human Practices, with the overcoming of Profession by Professionalism, with the overcoming of Praying by Prayers and with the overcoming of Principles by Party, has been separated from his God - a castaway in deed and in truth.

To the Minister, the words of Paul ring out, *'Take heed therefore unto yourselves, and to all the flock, over which the Holy Ghost hath made you overseers, to feed the church of God, which he hath purchased with his own blood.'* Acts 20:28.

Amen and Amen

9 World empires crash
but God remaineth

A SERMON PREACHED IN THE MARTYRS MEMORIAL CHURCH IN 1991 AFTER THE CRASH OF THE USSR AND THE RESIGNATION OF PRESIDENT GORBACHEV. THIS SERMON WAS LISTED BY A NATIONAL DAILY NEWSPAPER AS ONE OF THE TEN MOST STRIKING SERMONS PREACHED ON THAT OCCASION.

IN THE WEEK ENDING 28th December, 1991 the anti-God Union of Socialist Soviet Republics (USSR) - the great Communist superpower, the colossus brought into being by Lenin and Stalin, toppled and fell and is no more. The hammer and sickle flag was lowered from the Kremlin.

President Gorbachev resigned, but when he resigned he was not really a President. The nation was no more. If ever a politician had a name to live and was dead, Gorbachev was that individual.

The world can hardly take it in. The people of the former Soviet Republic are still mystified and stunned at the speed of the toppling of this great superpower which made the world tremble.

I happen to believe, personally, that this came about through the prayers of the Underground Church. I was thinking today there is an Underground Church in Heaven. In Revelation chapter six, John saw the souls of them that were beheaded for the Word of God and the testimony which they held. Where were they? They were under the altar. The Underground Church in Heaven. They prayed, 'How long O Lord?' And God said, 'Wait a little while.'

That little while has come and gone as far as Communist Russia is concerned, and those prayers have been abundantly and miraculously answered. Of course, there were the prayers of the Underground Church here on earth and in Russia itself, offered by faithful, Bible-loving, God-fearing, Christ-exalting separated people. Those prayers were not in vain in the Lord. What nuclear weapons could not do, atomic bombs could not do, and the NATO authorities could not do, God did. No wonder we sang tonight,

> 'God moves in a mysterious way,
> His wonders to perform.
> He plants His footsteps in the sea,
> And rides upon the storm.'

I want to call your attention to some illustrations and then I want to lay down some lessons which we can draw from the great fact of the toppling of this super world power.

THE FACT OF PHYSICAL CHANGE

Physical change is very easily discerned. Jet black hair grows grey and then turns white. You behold that when you look in the mirror. Is that not right? If it has not happened yet it is going to happen. So let me give you due and timely warning, that is if you can hold on to your hair! Some folks have trouble holding on to it.

The power of the arm grows weak. It is easily discerned, is it not? Youth passes on to maturity and maturity to old age, with all its consequence of decay and weakness. The once straight-as-a-ramrod man now bends his back and totters towards the grave.

In many cases the mind, so closely linked with the decaying body, also decays. We talk about people having their second childhood.

There is no doubt that physical change is easily discerned. It happens and it has happened and it will happen.

CHANGE IN THE WORLD OF NATURE

In the world of nature there seems to be a difference. Return to the place of your upbringing. The topography of the landscape, it seems, remains unchanged. The sun still rises over the hill or the mountain that is there, and still sets as it set in the days of your boyhood or girlhood. The moorland and the meadow seem to wear the same garments as they wore when you were a child.

The river runs in its well made bed and finds its way down towards the sea or lake. Is it not so that the Pharaohs lie in their stony sepulchres and Moses lies in his unmarked grave, known only by God Himself, and the old River Nile still flows on as it flowed in the days of the Pharaohs and in the days of Moses the great prophet?

David was Israel's great king. He was also Israel's sweet Psalmist. He lies in a Zion tomb. His remains have crumbled to dust. His harp is broken in ten thousand fragments, but the Mount Salmon is still snow-crested as it was in David's boyhood, and the River Kedron still flows through Jehoshaphat's valley.

Yes, the Lake of Galilee is still as it was when the foot of Christ touched it and it became solid as marble as He walked upon its waters.

Nature does not seem to change, and yet we are told by the scientists and the men of knowledge that nature is changing. The features and form of old mother earth are slowing and most surely changing. There is a continual unstoppable change in nature.

The heavens are also changing. Go out and look at the stars and see the galaxies of the stars in the Milky Way. Did you ever notice that the stars, like the sun, rise and set. They move in the heavens, but there is one star that does not move - the Pole Star. It remains where it was, but who can say that it remains as it was?

WHAT THE BIBLE SAYS

The Bible has something to tell us about this change of nature. Psalm 102 verse 25-28 says:-

'*Of old thou hast laid the foundation of the earth: and the heavens are the work of thy hands. They shall perish, but thou shalt endure: yea, all of them shall wax old like a garment; as a vesture shalt thou change them, and they shall be changed: But thou art the same, and thy years shall have no end. The children of thy servants shall continue and their seed shall be established before thee.*'

It is true, nature has changed, is changing and will yet change.

THE CHANGES IN THE POLITICAL WORLD

What about the world, not of the physical or natural but of politics?

Look over the political world and see how it has changed. Go down to the library and get a map of Europe pre the First World War. You will see countries marked on that map which you have never heard of. They have now disappeared forever from the map of Europe. Get a map of Europe after 1918 and compare it with pre-1914 and you will see the extent of change in Europe.

The world empire of Babylon, what happened to it? It crashed. The world empire of Persia, what happened to it? It crashed. The world empire of Greece, what happened to it? It crashed. The world empire of Rome, what happened to it? It crashed.

Leaders fall, leaders that made the world tremble, they fall. They were terrible in their lives, even more terrible in their deaths but they are gone.

The Kaiser thought he could ride astride the world but he came to a sorry and quick end. Hitler thought he could ride astride the world but he came to a quick end. The Communists under Lenin and Stalin thought they could ride astride the world but the USSR is no more. Its President found himself redundant. He had to close down his office and walk away from his chair of authority.

Think of the claims which the Communists made.

THE COMMUNIST FOLLY

I picked up a book which I have in my study, and I noticed that when the first Russian satellite touched outer space, Moscow's magazine indicated, and I quote what they said, 'Creation from a Communist point of view is at last under new management.'

The Communists claimed the prerogative of God. They claimed that they, not God, proposed and disposed. What fools they were!

Turn back to that Psalm 102 and emphasise the following parts. Look at what it says,

'*Of old* **Thou** *hast laid the foundation of the earth and the heavens are the work of Thy hands.* **They shall perish, but Thou shalt endure.**'

Write it in letters of gold. Let the world hear it. God endures. Empires crash, world leaders fall but our God endures. Look at the Psalm again,

'*As a vesture shalt* **Thou** *change them*' (v 26)

What is the power behind all these changes? Who is Sovereign outworking His plan, His programme and His purposes? God Almighty is Sovereign, He makes the changes. He rings them in and rings them out.

Look at verse 27, 'But **Thou** art the same.'
Child of God get the hold of this Eternal Truth - the Sameness of God. He is the same yesterday, He is the same today, and He is the same forever. Go back to my text in Lamentations and what does it say? 'Thou O Lord remaineth forever, Thy Throne from generation to generation.'

GOD REMAINETH

How glad I am this night that God remains! How glad I am I have a God Who cannot lie, and a God, Hallelujah, who cannot die! How glad I am that the Lord sitteth King forever! That word in the Hebrew for 'remain' means 'He sits undisturbed forever.' Nothing disturbs our God. Psalm 2.

How God laughed when the Communists wrote that piece in their Magazine that 'Creation was at last under new management.'

Where is the new management today? The Office of the President, the programme and the government, fallen and are no more! 'From everlasting to everlasting Thou art God.'

There was a great preacher who once said:-
'God has one telescope, and that telescope is His Omniscience, He sees everything, He is the all-knowing God.'

Our God Who remains King forever is the all-knowing God, unlimited in His knowledge, for He Himself is the Creator of all knowledge, and all knowledge is but a revelation of Himself. All that men may know and think and study and investigate are only the manifestation of God's created power. There is no knowledge, no true knowledge but what comes from God.

'But God has also one bridge which He crosses over to everything, that bridge is His Omnipresence. He is everywhere present." There is not a place where God is not. Take the wings of the morning, fly to the uttermost parts of the earth, there God will be. Go down into Hell and make your bed in the depths of Hell, there God will find you. Ascend to the highest point in outer space and beyond it to the third heaven, and go away out into the celestial stratosphere of the immeasurable eternity, there is God. Yes, He is Omniscient, He has got the telescope that sees everything. He has one bridge that crosses over to everything.

'He also has one hammer, and with that hammer He builds everything, that is His Omnipotence, He has all power.'

CONSUMING FIRE AND CONSUMING LOVE

When I open this Book I find out that God is a consuming fire. When I read on in this Book I find out that God is love. That seems to be a terrible contradiction, does it not? God - a consuming fire, God absolute unlimited, everlasting love!

If you are in Christ you will know the answer, for in Christ God is love. Outside Christ He is a consuming fire. That is the very heart of the Gospel. Oh, let me say to you that our God is love in Jesus Christ. There is nothing more wonderful, more majestic and more glorious than John's Gospel chapter three and verse 16,

'For God so loved the world that He gave His only begotten Son, that whosoever believeth in Him should not perish but have everlasting life.'

God is love! The Great, the Terrible, the Majestic God of Heaven loves men, loves women, loves boys and girls, loves the world. That means that He loves you.

GETTING THE LOVE MESSAGE ACROSS

Mr. Moody said, ' I want people when they come to my Tabernacle in Chicago to remember that God is love.' So he put a sign above the pulpit, 'God is love.'

He lit it up with gaslights. One night an old drunkard came in and he thought there was a fire, and he said, 'There is a fire behind the pulpit.' A man touched him on the shoulder and said, 'If you were not drunk you could read what the fire says.' The man turned round in his stupor and said, 'Well what does the fire say?'

It says, 'God is love.' The man staggered out and down the sidewalk but he could not get away from it, 'God is love.' He went back to his bottle but he could not get away from it, 'God is love.' He went back to the den where he slept. He lay down but he could not get away from it, it was burning into his heart, 'God is love.' And Mr. Moody records that God put out His great arms of love and He picked up that poor drunken man, clasped him to his bosom, brought him to the Cross, washed him in His Son's crimson blood, and put the Holy Ghost in his heart.

When the man came back to the Church he was stone sober and he was able to read the text for himself. His testimony was this, 'It is true! It is true! It is true! God is love.'

IT IS TRUE

Friend, it is true! But it is also true that outside of Christ God is a consuming fire. Who are you? You are just a worm and so am I. Who are you? You are just a speck of dust and so am I. What are the nations? They are only a drop in a bucket. This Great, Eternal, Omnipotent, Omniscient God is of purer eyes than to behold iniquity. Oh God, how great Thou art!

To think of it, that men would lift their puny little fists and shake them in the face of Deity! Oh, my friend in that chapter which we have quoted we not only read about a reigning God. How wonderful it is that He sits King forever, from generation to generation. He is the reigning God, but there is something else, it states that God is a God of wrath. 'Thou art very wroth against us.' And sinner, Christ-rejecting, Christ-reviling, Christ-crucifying sinner, God is a God of consuming fire. What is He going to be in your heart tonight? A God of Infinite love or a God of infinite wrath?

I am glad that there is an eye that never sleeps beneath the wing of night. There is an ear that never shuts when sinks the beams of light. There is an arm that never tires when human strength gives way. There is a love that never fails when earthly loves decay, and that is the love of God for sinners, and the love of God for you.

THE BANNER OF LOVE

D. L. Moody told of an incident during the Cuban civil war of 1867. An Englishman amongst them was tried as a spy, convicted and condemned to be shot. The American and the English ministers remonstrated with the Cuban authorities pointing out that he was innocent, but in vain. The time for the execution was fixed. The muskets of the soldiers were aimed at him, when the English and American ministers galloped up on horses, dismounted and wrapped the flags of their nations around the prisoner shouting to the Cuban soldiers, 'Fire on our flags if you dare!' They did not fire.

Make sure the Banner of the Saviour's love is wrapped around you. Thrice happy is the soul who can say, 'His banner over me is love.'

Amen and Amen

10 The big bang *versus the big God*

A SERMON PREACHED IN SEPTEMBER 1992 IN THE MARTYRS MEMORIAL CHURCH AFTER THE PRONOUNCEMENT BY SCIENTISTS THAT THE WORLD WAS CREATED BY A BIG BANG.

THE FIRST CHAPTER OF the Bible - the first chapter of the Book of Genesis and verse one states: *'In the beginning God created the heaven and the earth'*.

If you would like a title for my subject I would call it 'The Big Bang of the Scientists versus the Big God of the Scriptures'. If you would want the Scientists' text I would say 'In the beginning Bang'. If you would like the Scriptural text I would say 'In the beginning God'.

SCIENCE SO-CALLED

Man, puny but proud; man, scientific but sinful; man, advanced but retarded, has blown once again his tiny trumpet of self-congratulation and adoration, and has pontificated that he at long last, by his 'great' intelligence, by his 'infinite' wisdom, by his 'painstaking' research, has solved the mystery of the universe.

The message is this: *'The men of science are in their laboratories, let all the earth be silent before them'*.

I am sure you have read the Papers. *'The Independent'* 24/4/92 has a new start to its Bible. *'How the universe began, carefully wonderfully and meticulously charted'*.

It announces the heat that took place at a certain point fifteen billion years ago (I will come to this later). Fantastic that what happened fifteen billion years ago, they have been able to calculate the temperature of for us now. They claim what the barometer reading was; but, they have done more than that, they have told us what happened down to a fraction of a second after this so-called big bang.

It may surprise you to know that Quark soup was produced! Nothing to do with Scotch porridge. It is a new type of scientific cereal known as Quark soup. You, of course, are expected to be silent when these great men of science use such staggering language and make such stupendous and colossal claims.

I was watching television on the night of 23/4/92 and I heard one of the scientists proclaiming that they now know the secret, they have solved the riddle, they know exactly the timing of the beginning of the universe.

Are they all agreed? No! the Astronomer Royal says *'It could be pure codswallop'*. That is what he said. Another scientist says he cannot accept the theory, *'that as we started with a big bang we are going to disappear with a big bang'*. But let not the stupid people of this world be worried they say, for that second big bang is not going to come for another twenty million years. So they claim.

I want you to understand that they have it exact. They do not talk about fractions of millions or fractions of billions, but they have it exactly all neatly rounded off. It all works out in neat figures except when it comes to seconds. Then they go in for the minutiae of seconds.

THE RAM'S HORN

It is my purpose to take down the rugged unadorned ram's horn of Truth and to blow a blast upon that ram's horn, and when I have finished I believe this edifice - this edifice that has behind it the genius of Unbelieving, Godless, Christless, Truthless so-called science, will tumble as the walls of old Jericho did tumble many years ago.

Over against the scientists saying *'We are in our laboratories, let all the earth be silent before us'*, I would say, *'But the Lord is in His Holy Temple: let all the earth keep silent before Him'*. Hab. 2:20.

Let us open the only Book on earth that claims to be, and by its unity, its credibility, its authenticity, its impregnability and potency has proved itself to be the Word of God. Let us open it and let us read its first sentence again:- *'In the beginning God created the heavens and the earth'*.

Put over against that majestic, that sovereign, that musical anthem with which the Holy Book commences, words like this:- *'A N.A.S.A. spacecraft has detected echoes of the galaxy's birth fourteen thousand million years ago. The discovery about the formation of the universe after Big Bang has been hailed by excited scientists as 'the Holy Grail of Cosmology'*.

You know, when you put the sublime, the sovereign, the majestic, simple statement of the opening words of the Bible against that statement, you know that one has a ring of certainty, credibility and authority about it, and the other is the mere supposition of man.

There is no other book which commences with such a statement.

There is no other book which continues that theme and concludes it in almost similar words, *'I saw a new heaven and a new earth; for the first heaven and the first earth had passed away'* Revelation 21:1.

DR. JOSEPH PARKER'S COMMENT

When I was a young lad, and that is many years ago, I bought for the large sum of six pence, a book. It was written by a great Victorian preacher, Dr. Joseph Parker. Its title is *'None Like It'*, a reference to what David said of Goliath's sword, 'There is none like it, give it me'. It has this sub-title, *'A Plea for the Old Sword'*.

When I read this book there were a couple of paragraphs which fastened themselves into my mind. I never forgot them. I must have read this book over forty years ago, but today I went to my library. It is a very big library, containing, I suppose, about 12,000 books. I pulled out this book and turned up the very page and I read it again. I want to read it to you, because it is, I believe, the finest comment ever made on that great declaration: *'In the beginning God created the heaven and the earth'*.

Parker says:-

'In the first verse of the Bible I find the message of the whole volume. That first verse may be represented in various ways; as a manner of announcement it is sudden thunder; as a revelation it is morning dawning through gathered darkness; as an answer to mute but hopeful wonder it is like the sunrise on the sea. This is Infinite speech, *'In the beginning God created the heavens and the earth'*.

Taken as a mere sentence can it be exceeded in grandeur? Taken as an Inspired thought who can heighten its elevation? Taken as a direct voice from Eternity who can charge it with apology or incertitude? If this sentence is not the very Word of God I dare not, I can not, I will not say it is the word of man.

Let us listen: *'In the beginning'*. the remotest date that has yet been suggested. Science has its slow rising and slow falling centuries yet the beginning - the dateless date includes them all and drowns them in a deeper sea. On that ocean, millenniums are tufts of foam.

God, - Personality, Will, Thought, Purpose and Undefined Definition matching the unbeginning Beginning, Personality the shapeless shape, God, He enters His own Book instantaneously, He comes not as a spectacle but in the very Glory of His Divine Purpose.

Created, - a process slow, quick, deliberate, infinite, before all speech therefore baffling speech; before all forms therefore without comparison; the beginning of action - action without parallel.

Man, - never spoke this word of his own volition, he was told to speak it. Eternity delivered the secret to him and whispered it in every syllable. There is no mark of man upon it. It is a planet man never moulded. It is the Morning Star.'

THE START OF THE BIBLE

Note with me that the Bible does not start with an explanation, it starts with pure revelation. The Bible does not make its first verse an argument, it makes its first verse an announcement. God enters His Book as He is.

No wonder the patriarch Moses raised his voice in song. No wonder his sister Miriam took up her timbrel and joined in that song. The heart of that song was this: *'Who is like unto Thee, O, Lord, among the gods? Who is like unto Thee, glorious in holiness, fearful in praises, doing wonders?'* Exodus 18:11

The Lord Jesus Christ stood amongst a bunch of critics as He performed on earth His duties of preaching in the days of His Humiliation. If you turn in the Bible to the fifth chapter of John's Gospel you will read that the Saviour said, in verse 46 of that chapter: *'For had ye believed Moses, ye would have believed me'*.

I say to these Godless scientists, I say to these Christless scholars, I say to those so puffed up in their own self-declared intelligence and genius that they close their eyes to the One Who is Truth Incarnate, *'If ye had believed Moses ye would have believed Christ'*.

The heavens, what do they do? They declare the glory of God. They do not declare the glory of the Big Bang. They declare the glory of the Big God. *'The heavens declare the glory of God, the firmament sheweth His handiwork'* Psalm 19:1. Why can't men of science, so-called, see it? I will tell you why, because they have in their folly put out their own eyes in their unbelief, and having jettisoned God from their thoughts, they set out to jettison God from His own universe. The Bible says, *'The fool in his heart says, There is no God'.*

ROMANS CHAPTER ONE

Look at the first chapter of Romans verse nineteen. What a passage it is! You will notice that in it we read, *'Because that which may be known of God is manifest in them; For God hath shewed it unto them'.*

In every man's heart there is the innate knowledge that God is. Nowhere in the world, in any generation has there been found any tribe or people or any nation that did not worship. Of course, in their sins they worship falsely. In the darkness of a conscience which also is deformed and debauched by the fall of man they know not the truth. But every created man and begotten man is a worshipper. Why? Because the innate knowledge of God, even with all man's fall, has not been erased from his soul.

We all have a conscience. It either accuses us or excuses us. That conscience is governed by a law - the law of right and wrong.

Was it a Big Bang fifteen billion years ago which produced that law? Was it some strange freak of some sort of atmospheric conditions in outer space some fifteen billion years ago that wrote into every man yet to come and inhabit this planet, the law of the right and the law which exposes wrong?

What does the Book say? The Book says, *'Because that which may be known of God is manifest'* Where? *'In them; for God hath shewed it unto them'.*

There is a manifestation within every man's heart, in his conscience. There is also a manifestation outside man entirely divorced from man and separated from him. What is that? That is the great Creation. Look at verse 20:-

'For the invisible things of him from the creation of the world'.

From that dateless date *'In the beginning,'* the invisible things of God are clearly seen. They are not blurred. Here we have men who claim to have great knowledge. No one doubts, as far as data is concerned, and no one doubts, as far as multiplicity of propositions are concerned, they have great knowledge. As far, however, as being prepared to admit the truth, they are in darkness. Yet these things *'are clearly seen being understood by the things that are made'* God's creation, God's making. And what are these things that are clearly seen? What are these things that are reflected in God's making? His Eternal power and Godhead!

LEARN FROM THE MOTOR CAR

Go and look at a motorcar. Do you think it grew out of the pavement or the roadway or the street? Do you? Do you think that that thing just suddenly happened? There was a Big Bang somewhere and a motorcar appeared. Workmanship presupposes a workman. It presupposes something else. It presupposes that that workman must have had the ability, must have had the intelligence, must have had the power, must have had the 'know-all' to produce the workmanship.

If I stood beside you outside the motorcar and I told you it just happened, you would say to the driver: *'Take him to the asylum, do not take him to the hotel, he is dangerous'.*

I have heard people say *'Oh, you must believe it, these are clever men. You must accept it, after all you are not a scientist'*. No, thank God, I am more scientific to be a so-called *scientist.*

O GOD, HOW GREAT THOU ART!

God has given to ordinary people His Word, and in this Word we are instructed that His Eternal power and Godhead are manifested clearly in His works.

I stood some time ago at the Great Divide in the Rockies. I saw the towering Rocky Mountains on either side, and as I stood there I said in my heart, *'How great Thou art!'* There was beauty there. There was majesty there. There was the silence that spoke in a still small voice to my heart. How I thanked God I had the submissiveness to say *'Not unto us, but unto Thy Great Name be the Glory'.*

I came over once in a plane from the United States of America. I might as well have been in a row boat. It was the worst crossing I ever experienced, and the worst crossing that the crew and the pilot and all the passengers ever experienced.

That plane, a large jumbo jet, was like a kite. I had a young man with me and it was one of his first flights. He held on frantically to the seat in front of him until his hands were white. He thought that if he held on to the seat all would be well. What was the use of holding on to a seat at 33,000 feet up? It was not much good! I did the best thing. I went to sleep, that is what I did. You can do nothing in such circumstances but believe. I had faith that if it was God's will for me to return I would return. If it was not God's will for me to return, my body would perish but my redeemed spirit would go higher than 33,000 feet. It would go to the place where the everlasting Lord dwells, to take its position through grace alone, through pardon alone, through the Blood of Christ alone, among that multitude which no man can number.

As that plane rocked about I said to myself *'I'm glad my Heavenly Father controls the storm'. How insignificant we all are!*

I want to tell you, all the cleverness of these scientists, if they were up in that jet and God blew His winds, all their knowledge of Big Bangs and Quark soup would not do them much good, would it?

People often say, when some man is killed, *'What a waste!'* Of course I understand what they are saying, but life is not limited by the boundaries of birth and death.

Your life has no limitation in its continuation. That is why it is more important to prepare for the future which will far exceed your short pilgrimage in time. We are made for Eternity.

When I survey the universe, when I look at it there is to me a harmony and a unity and a beauty which cannot be denied. Materialism may chant about certain laws which go into action. I would ask the materialist, 'But whose laws are these? And by whose power do they operate?' A law must have a force behind it to implement it. What is the use of Parliament making a law if the security forces cannot put that law into operation.

LORD KELVIN

These scientists (and the Press has been filled with their speech this week) are what the Bible calls 'so-called scientists', because true science deals with facts not with fancies, with proofs not with presumptions, and with truths not theories.

Lord Kelvin was undoubtedly one of the greatest thinkers in the scientific field at the end of the last century. He wrote a striking letter to The Times, and in that letter he had some most interesting things to say. Let me read to you just a brief extract: *'Was there anything so absurd as to believe that a number of atoms by falling together of their own accord could make a sprig of moss a microbe - a living animal? It is utterly absurd. Here scientific thought is compelled to accept creative power. Forty years ago I asked Liebig, who was one of the great scientists of his day, if he believed that the grass and the flowers which we saw around us grew by mere mechanical force. The great scientist replied: 'No more than I could believe that a book of botany describing them could grow by such a force. Let them not imagine that any hocus-pocus of electricity or viscous fluids would make a living cell...Nothing approaching to a cell of living creature has ever yet been made...No artificial process whatever could make living matter out of dead."*

It is utter absurdity and nonsense to pretend that chance can do it all.

The suggestion was once put to a so-called scientist if we could get a hundred typewriters and let loose upon them a hundred chimpanzees to dance on them, would it be possible to produce accurately the entire works of Shakespeare? And the scientist said *'Yes'*. An ordinary common man in the street said *'No'*. The scientist was a fool and the ordinary man was a wise man. Yet we are told that out of say one thousand million chances the one chance happened in a Big Bang fifteen billion years ago.

You are sitting with the intelligence that you have because the Bang went the right way. Who is going to believe that? Only a fool would believe that. No wonder I say that these scientists' autobiography is:-

'Once I was a tadpole beginning to begin;
Then I became a frog, with my tail tucked in;
Then a monkey up a banyon tree;
Now a professor with a Ph.D.'

They ask sensible, common decent folk, to whom God has given a degree of grey matter between their ears, to swallow hook, line and sinker, what they say.

THE GREAT TIME CLOCK

I would like to ask some of these scientists tonight, 'Do you really expect us to accept that you are giants and every one else is only a pygmy? That your brain is of such a developing nature that you have left all your fellows behind? You expect us to look at something that is nonsensical and bow the knee and say, 'We must believe you'.

I ask, 'Where did you get this time clock? You have produced its results in your chart. This is a time clock which measures back some fifteen billion years, and measures not only years in billions of years and thousands of years but also measures to a fraction of a second. Now in this chart when this Big Bang, which you claim took place, you actually tell us what happened at 10.43 seconds, and then what happened at 10.34 seconds after the so-called Big Bang.'

'Think of that. That is some time clock, is it not? You certainly get down to the smallest fraction of time, do you not? Yes, right down to the very fraction of it. Do you mean to tell me that you, a scientist, have a time clock that can only go back fifteen billion years and measure to the tiniest fraction of a second and postulate or *pontificate* would be a better word, what happened between those split seconds?'

One comment in the article is *'It was a bit like porridge, it was lumpy.'* So there you are. My mother was a Scotch woman, she believed in feeding her sons on porridge - she taught me how to make porridge, and she used to say 'Stir it well, for it will be lumpy if you do not stir it'.

Evidently this Big Bang produced the universe, produced all the generations of all men and women of all ages, had not enough wit to make the porridge non-lumpy. It could not stir the porridge. No wonder it produced what the scientists log as *'Quark soup'*.

It goes on to talk about what happened in one second. *'In one second, stable subnuclear particles, neutrons and protons were formed'*. Think of it! In one second! It goes on to say that the date to be remembered from the Big Bang is 300,000 years. Then there was the epoch of *'re-combination, the first ripples of cosmic structure'*. After that, over fourteen billion years had to pass *'before the molecule of inheritance began and life on earth started to emerge'*.

THE GREAT BAROMETER

When I look at the other side of the chart I find they not only have a time clock but they have a barometer.

This barometer measures' up to 10.32 degrees centigrade and it goes down to -270 degrees centigrade. *When the first life on earth began to emerge the temperature was -270 degrees centigrade'*. These must have been a frosty lot! But when the Big Bang took place the barometer measured 10.32 degrees centigrade above. It took billions of years on one side of the chart to produce life. It took billions of years to produce this rapid fall in temperature to -270 degrees.

I would say to these scientists, *'Do you actually think that any sensible man would believe that after fifteen billion years you are able to do this?'*

THE GREAT CAMERA

That is not the whole story. They now tell us in this article that this spaceship, *'this satellite camera called Coba (listen to this) has taken a snapshot of the universe just three hundred thousand years after Big Bang itself!'* It has gone back into time. We read of space trips, but here is the most wonderful space trip! This camera was able to go back to three hundred thousand years after the Big Bang so it has gone back almost fifteen billion years and miraculously it has produced a snapshot. The Astronomer Royal says we should not shout too loudly about this. *'The scientific community must examine the results before shouting too loudly about their importance, for the dust between the stars can also produce this ripple'*. The dust between the stars could do that, and it could be that what they are seeing is ripples from the radiation of dust between the stars, and nothing whatsoever to do with what they say their photograph portrays. Then he goes on to say, (I notice it is not reported in *The Independent*, for *The Independent* seems to think that all the scientists say is true) *'It is either the discovery of the decade, or pure codswallop'* - The words of the Royal Astronomer!

A GODLESS, CHRISTLESS THEORY

I find my intelligence far pushed to think that the common people of our country are going to accept this. Think with me for a moment what it means. It means this, that there is no God. This is a Godless theory. This theory has come forth from the womb of antagonistic atheism to the very thought of the Being of God. If this universe started with a Big Bang there is no hope, there is no gospel, there is no eternal life, there is nothing. This Bible is a cheat. Christ is an impostor and God does not exist.

I happen to believe that God does exist - God is. I happen to believe that Christ is the Way, the Truth and the Life. I happen to believe that the Bible, though burned, survived its burnings; though attacked has survived its attacks; though buried has had innumerable resurrections, and the old Book still stands, and will stand and when this codswallop is forgotten the old Bible will remain standing.

There was a great philosopher in Aberdeen some years ago called Dr. Beattie. He was also a very sincere Christian. When his young son grew up he taught him to read. Once the boy was able to read his name, his father went out into the garden one morning and with his finger he spelt the boy's name on a plot that had just been dug and was ready for seed. He then took in his hand some mustard and cress seeds and sowed them along the channels that formed the letters of the boy's name. In due time the mustard and cress grew.

One day his boy came into his father's study and said *'Father, somebody has done something in the garden, my name is growing there'*. The father laughed and said, *'Son, do not be stupid'* The son said, *'Come and see'* So he took his father out and there, sure enough, was his name growing in mustard seed. He looked at his boy, *'Ach'* he said, *'that just came by chance, son'*. The boy looked at him and said, *'Father, that could not have come by chance, somebody did that. That is there because somebody made the channel and sowed the seed'*.

His father looked at him, and said, *'That is right my son, there must be an adequate cause to produce this effect'*. Then he said *'I want you to look at something more wonderful than your name. I want you to look at the wonderful person that name stands for. I want to tell you, my boy, you are fearfully and wonderfully made. It was not man that made you, you are a creature of God. God made the first man and the first woman, and you, my boy, are God's handiwork'*.

THE ANSWER IS GOD

Let me say, that simple truth which Dr. Beattie taught his son explodes forever these myths and lies. God is a God Who doeth wonders. He doeth wonders in creation but He doeth wonders in maintaining what He has created.

Let me take you out and show you a giant oak tree. Its roots are far into the ground, almost as much in the ground as above the ground, or perhaps at times even more.

It has a fibre of bark that is tough and can stand up to all weathers. Its wood itself is tough and hard. Look at that mighty oak.

Let me, however take a little acorn and put it into your hand. I can put it into the tiny hand of the tiniest child, and that child is holding in its tiny little hand the potential of that great giant oak tree. It is all in that little acorn.

It just happened because there was a Big Bang. I hope you know that that is how it happened! Nobody designed it. Nobody made that acorn different from the seedling of any other tree. It all just happened'.

'In the Beginning chance'? No, 'In the beginning God' 'In the beginning God'

In the beginning of time, God. In the beginning of man, God. In the beginning of earth, God. In the beginning of the heavens, God. In the beginning of Salvation, God. In the beginning of redemption, God. In the beginning of grace, God. In the beginning of the Gospel, God.

When the earth emerged from the swaddling clothes of the mists of the first morning, we can see emblazoned across the first revealed horizon, God. Survey history and you will see God. Peer into the future and there is God. Look back to the beginning, He is there. When the great climax comes and there is an end that never ends, God will still be presiding and His Throne will still be ruling over all. God is Central, Supreme, Sovereign, and praise His Name, Saving. Like the old prophet who said, 'I will hide myself 'till my time is come', so I will go to Genesis chapter one and verse one, 'In the beginning God' and I will hide myself there 'till my time is come'.

JOSEPH PARKER AGAIN

I commenced this message by quoting old Joseph Parker, let me finish it by quoting him again.

'What God creates, God protects. What God protects, God redeems. What God redeems, God prizes, and what God prizes, God completes'.

I have news for you tonight, God did not start building the tower and then leave off half way through. God will complete His work. God did not start down the furrow and then forsake the plough mid furrow. God will complete the score.

Christ, we read, is the image of the Invisible God, the firstborn of every creature. Creation predicates redemption. Redemption predicates resurrection. Resurrection predicates ascension, and ascension predicates Glory, and thank God, the Blood predicates the forgiveness of sins.

'In the beginning, God,' my loving, Sovereign, Saving, Sustaining God, I believe in the Son of God to the salvation of my soul.

Unsaved one, I say to you, Believe on the Lord Jesus Christ Who through the Eternal Spirit offered Himself without spot unto God, and thou shalt be saved.

In the beginning, it is God. In the end it is God. When death calls us away we will go to God, if we are washed in the Blood of the Lamb. Let us turn from the theories of men to the Truth of God. Let us turn from the presumptions of men to the mighty proofs of our All Mighty God.

Amen and Amen

11 Swearing allegiance
to King Jesus

A SERMON PREACHED ON LORD'S DAY 24TH MARCH, 1991 TO SOME 12,000 PEOPLE IN THE KINGS HALL, BELFAST ON THE 40TH ANNIVERSARY OF THE FOUNDING OF THE FREE PRESBYTERIAN CHURCH OF ULSTER. THE TEXT WAS I CHRONICLES 12:18 "THINE ARE WE, DAVID, AND ON THY SIDE, THOU SON OF JESSE."

IN THIS HISTORIC EVENT recorded in this passage of Scripture, David was an exile. He had been forced out of his own country into the enemy's territory - the land of the Philistines. He had been banished. He was reviled and rejected, though anointed king of Israel.

His followers were few. His critics were many and his enemies numerous, yet in this time of exile and banishment, misrepresentation, revilement and ridicule, these men came, some of them from the tribe of Benjamin. As you will notice in verse 16, that was the tribe of Saul the arch enemy of David, and they came to lonely, persecuted, reviled, hated, banished and exiled David and said, *'Thine are we, David, and on thy side, thou son of Jesse.'*

THE PARALLEL

It is not hard to draw the parallel is it? I know that my Saviour is exalted. I know He sits at God's right hand expecting the Lord to make His enemies lick the dust at His feet. I know that Heaven's anthems ring out across the vast immeasurable expanses of heaven the praises of the Lamb - for the Lamb is all the glory in

Emmanuel's land. But down here on earth the Lord is exiled. He is banished. He is rejected. He is reviled. He is criticised. He is hated.

Not many rally to His defence. Not many want to be associated with Him. Not many want to bear His reproach and go outside the camp to where He is. Not many want to run the gauntlet of a satanic world that hates the Bible, that hates the Blood, that hates the old Book and hates the Lord Jesus Christ.

Could I say to you, it was a religious crowd that got Jesus to the Cross. It was a religious crowd that buffeted and beat Him and spat upon Him in the Jewish place of leadership. And the religious crowd today, men and women, still bays for the Blood of Jesus Christ.

Where is the Lord Jesus Christ? He is not in the Vatican, He is not in Canterbury, He is not in the World Council of Churches - they hate Him, they fight Him, they defame Him and they reject Him.

Old Sandy Peden the Scottish Covenantor said, 'Where is the Kirk of Scotland today? Not in the great Cathedrals, not in the established Church. The Kirk of Scotland is where a praying lad or lassie, separated from religious apostasy, kneels down and prays in the Name of Jesus. There at the dykeside, on the mountain, among the heather, that is where the Kirk of Scotland is.'

Where is the Church of Jesus Christ in Ulster? It is outside the camp, and I am glad I am outside the camp. A BBC man said to me before this service, 'What will happen in forty years?' I said, 'I will not be responsible forty years hence, but I pray that God will send a young Joshua to bring this Church into the Promised Land - a land flowing with milk and honey.'

I am only responsible for my own ministry and my own day and generation and I am responsible to prepare men to stand for God. What they do is their responsibility - but I do not think that God is going to forsake this church. I do not think it depends on man. I do not think it depends on any human leader. I do not think it depends on any talents. It does not depend on anything we have,

God in the midst of her doth dwell,
Nothing shall her remove,
The Lord to her a helper will,
And that right early prove

ONE: THE EXAMPLE TO BE EMULATED

There are three things to be looked at in this text. **First there is an example to be emulated.** What did these men do? It says here that they came to David. That is the first thing you have to do, you have to come to Jesus Christ.

As a boy of six years old on 29th May, 1932 I came to Jesus Christ. I have the old pew that I knelt at (I do not believe in relics but I believe in precious memories) and down in our college I have that pew out of the old Baptist Church in Hill Street, Ballymena where I knelt as a lad and I came to Jesus, and thank God, He took me in.

I did not know very much but I knew this, that I was a sinner. I knew that Christ died for sinners and I knew if I came to Christ he would not cast me out. That is the Gospel, that is all you need to know, sinner, and if you have never come to Christ, come today.

Somewhere in this hall is there some man, some woman, with a burden of sin in their heart? Some young person who is struggling with deep battles within their soul? I tell you what to do, come to Jesus, that is what to do.

No Church can save, no sacrament can save, no religion can save but Jesus saves to the very uttermost - from the guttermost to the uttermost - all that come unto Him.

MOTIVATED BY DAVID'S PAST

That is the first thing these men did in the text, they came. They came because they were motivated by three things. **Number one, they were motivated by David's past.** They had heard about David. They heard of his manner and his person. They heard that he was a prince among men. They heard he would be marked among thousands and tens of thousands, that there was something special about him, something that set him apart from other men.

Yes, I have heard about the Lord Jesus. I have heard that he is the fairest of ten thousand, that he is the rose of Sharon, that he is the Bright and Morning Star, and that none like Him can be found anywhere among the sons of men.

Have we not heard about Jesus? Have we not heard about the wonder of His Person, the Majesty of His countenance, the tender compassion of His eye, the gloriousness of His manner, the graciousness of His speech, and the wonder of His love?

They heard about David. They had heard about his person. They had also heard about his battles. They heard that one day the whole of Israel had been put to shame before the uncircumcised Goliath. That Saul trembled, that Jonathan trembled. That both had been mighty men of war but now cowardice had come and their strong bloodstream had thinned and they ran from the enemy. They had heard for forty days Goliath had held the God of Heaven up to ridicule and had put shame upon every true Israelite of God. They had heard about a young man who came from the sheepfold - a young man with a sling. He went out alone and he defied the giant, and he laid him low, and he took off his head and God won for Israel a great victory.

Have you not heard of the great giant of Hell who came out and reviled mankind? Have you not heard how every man had thin blood? There was not found among the sons of men any one who could take on the Beelzebub of the pit, the Satan of the underworld of damned spirits? Then there came One of ruddy countenance, the purity of His blood was seen in His very cheeks. There came One from the Hills of Glory, from His Father's House. There came One with love and compassion and grace in His breast and He went out and fought the great Goliath of the pit; He staggered up that bloody mountain - that Hill of Reproach called Calvary. He hung stark naked on an accursed tree, bearing shame and scoffing, but in His dying, He slew death. He destroyed him that had the power of death, that is to say the devil, and delivered them who through fear of death were all their lifetime subject to bondage.

We have heard about Him! We have heard about the great victory that He won. We have heard about Him!

MOTIVATED BY DAVID'S PRESENT

These men were also motivated by David's present. They saw him despised. They saw Saul campaigning for his life. They saw how the Princess Michal had been taken from him, for was he not son-in-law to the king? They saw this man fleeing across the wilderness and leaping from rock to rock on the mountainsides of the wilderness and upon the mountain places of Judea. They heard how Saul planned to take away his life. How Saul insisted that he must die, and how the men that should have stood by him - the men that he had befriended and helped and saved - had turned their back on him.

Have we not heard today of what the so called church has done with Jesus Christ? Have we not heard that in the General Assembly the vote was for Professor Davey and not for Jesus? And they voted that the man who said that Jesus Christ was illegitimate was their man. They rejected the Virgin born Son of God. When the man who said, 'There are literally thousands of inaccuracies in the Bible,' they said, ' Give us that man, we do not want the Bible.'

As Professor Haire said on that occasion, 'Our church never believed in an Infallible Bible.' He should read the Westminster Confession of Faith which he signed and swore to believe.

As W. P. Nicolson said, 'A hare was always an unclean animal in Scripture, you would not expect anything else from Professor Haire, would you?'

Let me say something to you, the Irish Presbyterian church said 'No' to Jesus.

When we went to Crossgar to preach the Gospel they said 'No' to Jesus. They said, 'You can have what you like in your Church Hall, we do not care what you have in there, but you will not have the Gospel.' We have heard about that, but we have come to stand by Jesus Christ, that is all we are doing here today, we are going to stand by him. When a man says, 'Jesus Christ is illegitimate,' I am going to roar at the top of my voice, 'Jesus is Virgin born, shut up you liar!' that is what we are going to do.

We did it in the Fair Hill in Ballymena very effectively when Donald Soper's soap opera came to a speedy end. I remember Rev. John Wylie and myself being in Court and fined £5 for disorderly behaviour! It was the best £5 worth I ever had. I will tell you something more, I never believed in paying a fine if I was innocent and we did not pay the fine, and I am eternally grateful and so is John Wylie to the Official Unionist Party who paid our fine for us. There was an election coming and they did not want John Wylie and Ian Paisley in jail so they said, 'Pay their fines.'

When these old modernistic apostates came to this land we have gone after them. Weatherhead, Soper, McCloud and all the rest of them. Why did we go after them? Because we wanted to stand up for Jesus. I want to tell you from this platform that as long as this Church exists and stands true we are going say to Christ, 'Thine are we, Jesus, and on Thy side, Thou Son of God.'

There is one thing you will never do in Heaven, you will never bear the reproach of Christ and if you have not borne it down here you have lost the joy that you would have got in the glory land. What did Moses say? He counted the reproaches of Christ greater riches than the treasures of Egypt, for he had respect unto the recompense of the reward.

I remember the first time I was in jail. The jail door closed and the lock turned and I was alone. I sat down on an old bed, it was not like the decent beds they have now in prison, it was an old hard bed, and the cell filled with the glory of God. I wept like a child. There was not one tear of sorrow, they were tears of joy, that I was counted worthy to suffer shame for Jesus' sake.

My friend, I invite you to say to Christ, 'Thine are we, Lord Jesus, and on Thy side, Thou Son of God, Thou persecuted Christ, Thou reviled Christ, Thou hated Christ, Thou Christ from whom men have taken Thy Spotless Birth and Sinless Life and Precious Blood and Wonderful Miracles.'

All these old apostates have gone through Jesus and tell you there is no Deity there. They have gone through the Bible and tell you there is no inspiration and no infallibility there. They have gone through the Gospel and they have told you there is no new birth there. They have gone through heaven and have told you there is no gold there and they have gone through hell and have told you there is no fire there. They have gone through God's message and have left it as a carcass without blood, without flesh, without bones and without life.

I believe there is Inspiration in the Bible. I believe there is Deity in Jesus. I believe there is power in the Blood of the Lamb. I believe there is gold in Heaven and fire in Hell, and I believe that the Gospel is a mighty Gospel that saves. This afternoon I say to you, let us get on the side of Jesus today. Let this King's Hall send the message to Heaven, 'Lord Jesus, we are on your side,' and if the way be rough, so be it. If the hatred increases ten thousand times, so be it. Is He not worth bearing reproaches for? Is He not worth living for and serving and even dying for?

MOTIVATED BY DAVID'S FUTURE

These men had heard about David's present but these men had also their eye on **David's future - his prospect.** They knew some day that David really would be King. They knew he would walk in the palace corridors of Zion. They knew that all over Israel from Dan to Bathsheba Saul would no longer be King, but this young man who had been anointed by old man Samuel with oil amidst his brethren, was going to be a King, what a King, a victorious King, a King that no man could fight and no man could beat, a King of kings, and they looked forward to that day and said, 'It may be rough going but we have our eyes on the future.'

I heard a preacher say one day that you should not get your eyes on rewards. What a foolish man he was! Moses had respect for the recompense of the reward. I would serve Jesus if there was no reward at the end, for serving Him is reward enough, but there is going to be a reward. Some day we are going to reign with Him, and you know I am an heir of God and a joint heir with Jesus. I am going to reign with Him. In the millennium reign He is going to set us over cities. Some people will have ten cities, some people will have two cities. I have asked God for two cities, I would settle for Rome and Dublin - that would do me!

Let me tell you, friend, we are going to reign with Him. I have got my eyes on the future, brethren, for the crowning day is coming. My Lord will not always be reproached and despised and rejected. Some day the trumpet will sound and the sepulchres of the righteous will be emptied, and there shall be change. They shall leave off the rags of mortality and put on immortality and they will leave off the dissolution of the dust and put on the robes of everlasting destiny and if we are living we shall be changed and together we shall be caught up to be with the Lord. What a day that is going to be! When I look on His face I will be glad I stood against old Soper and Weatherhead and every other brat of the Devil that says disparaging things against the Saviour. I will be glad I will be able to look Him in the eye and say, 'Lord Jesus, I was not much but when men hated you and despised you and put the Pope in your place, I stood against them.' I will be glad I will be able to say that, and I will be glad I am in a Church that takes such a stand.

I am sad today about the state of the churches in this land. They have all gone after the modern perversions of the Word of God. They have all gone after New Evangelicalism with emphasis on the 'jelly' and they are afraid to mention the Pope or Popery.

I heard a man preaching about a well known Protestant leader. He said he 'took a stand against erroneous doctrine,' afraid to say he was against the Pope. I am not afraid to say it and practise it. That is why this morning on the BBC you had an Irish Presbyterian minister and a priest in harmony against this church. Long may the apostates be in harmony with Popery, and let the people of Ulster know just where they stand. We know where we stand as Free Presbyterians. We will not give in one inch to Popery. We will not give in to this religion which puts a man in the place of the Godman; which puts a Pope in the place of Jesus; which puts a priest in the place of God the Holy Ghost. We reject his wafers, his confessional boxes, his holy water so-called, and holy beads and candle grease. We reject his Cardinals, his nuns and his friars and if he has any broilers we reject them as well!

That is where we stand. It is quite clear.

A fellow said to me today, 'In your younger days you were very outspoken.' I said, 'You are the first fellow who has told me that I am not outspoken today.' He said, 'I'm not just talking about today.' I said, 'Would you like me to say something outspoken on your Radio?'

The Church of Rome is still worshipping cast clouts and rotten rags. I got a letter from a Roman Catholic priest just the other day with a whole list of 'holy relics that can bring peace to your soul.' I was in Rome recently attending a political meeting of the European Parliament and I went into a place where they had a 'holy well that could heal everybody'. I saw many people coming but nobody was healed. You would just be as well with water out of the tap at home. The great delusion! I say to my Roman Catholic fellow countrymen, 'I am not saying something to insult your religion, I am trying to get you to the Lord Jesus Christ. He can save you. He can change you. He can transform you. You do not need to kneel at a confessional box before a bachelor priest who has more sins than you have and yet pretends to forgive you.'

It was C. H. Spurgeon who said that 'the priest is worse than the devil, for the devil has not even the cheek to say he can forgive your sins, and yet that black coated bachelor of Rome tells you he can forgive you your sins.' (Strong language!)

There is only One person who can forgive your sins and that is the Lord Jesus Christ.

I want to say to you today I am looking forward to the Coming of our Lord Jesus Christ!

TWO: THE EXAMINATION TO BE EMPHASISED

David does not receive these men immediately. The Lord does not receive you immediately when you say you are going to do battle for Him. He has to test you. You have to go through an examination and there is an examination here. David said, 'If ye become peaceable.'

There is no such thing as peace until evil is put away. First purity and then peace. We must be pure doctrinally if we are going to be at peace with the Lord. If you are at peace with Him you will know the purity of the cleansing Blood and you will know the purity of the mighty indwelling of the pure Spirit of God.

There were three men who came to Jesus and said, 'I will be your disciple,' but not one of them followed Him. One said, 'I will follow you.' Jesus said, 'Foxes have holes, the birds of the air have nests, the Son of man hath no where to lay His head.' The man did not follow Jesus.

I remember a young girl coming to Ravenhill Free Presbyterian Church. She was seventeen years old, she got converted and when she went home that night and told her parents they put her outside the door and locked it and said, 'We do not mind you being converted but if you attend Ian Paisley's church there is no home for you here.' That poor young girl in her teens came to tell us, 'I have been put out of my home.' Thank God, God had a home for her and praise God, although the Lord was right, 'Foxes have holes and the birds of the air have nests, but the Son of Man hath no where to lay His head,' that young woman was prepared to follow Christ.

In the early days of the Free Church we had a rough time you know. You could not buy a plot of ground. I could write story after story of how we got ground to build our churches. It would take the Encyclopaedia Brittanica to contain what I could write. I remember going to Armagh and the day we formed the church there the man who was a very good man and gave us the ground for our tent meetings, said, 'You can have it as long as you like.' I constituted a church and received something like 50 members. Then suddenly we had nowhere to go because the man came to the gate and when the Benediction was pronounced he said to me, 'You are out.' I asked 'Why?' and he said, 'I am not telling you.' I said, 'The pressures have been on you but it is all right, we will be out.'

There was a bit of ground in the Mall between the old Masonic Hall and the First Presbyterian Church and a friend of mine who belongs to the Church of God said to me, 'Ian, if you want a bit of ground there is a bit of ground there, it is not big but you could get some sort of a building erected there.' So I bought a portable hall of a Plymouth brother evangelist and went down to erect this hall on this ground. I left the men to do the work but when I got to Belfast there was a phone message, 'Come quickly, you are in trouble.' When I got down the Chief of police (they called them District Inspectors in those days) was there along with the Chairman of the Council and the Town Clerk. Before I left Belfast I got in touch with a very learned lawyer and asked what to do. He said, 'Ian if they are on your property they are trespassing, throw them off.' So I went down and thought, " it will give me great pleasure to throw them off!"

They were right on my property and my men had stopped their work. I said, 'Men, get started, you go and build that hall and I will handle these three musketeers.'

I looked at them and said, 'D.I. what are you doing on my property?' I asked the Council Chairman, 'What are you doing on my property?' He said, 'Paisley, there will never be a Free Presbyterian Church in Armagh.' I said, 'Are you threatening me?' He said, 'You can take it whatever way you like, there will never be a Free Presbyterian Church in Armagh.' I said, 'You are the Chairman of the Council, which is the statutory planning authority. I take it that you are using your authority to stop any planning application I put in. I will keep that against you and it will be good ammunition when it comes to an appeal. You are bigoted and biased.'

I turned to the Town Clerk and asked, 'Town Clerk what are you doing here?' He said, 'Oh, I am here with the Chairman.' I said, 'Now you have two minutes to get off this site.' They said, 'We are not getting off, we are going to stop this hall being built.' I said, 'I have just to call those men and they are going to throw you off. Now D.I. you are trespassing.' He blinked and said, 'I suppose technically I am.' I said, 'Would you please get these men off the site.' He said, 'Gentlemen you know he is right.' I smiled a big broad Paisley grin and I said, 'Yes, I am in the right, now off you go.' They got out and they stood on the street and they told me what they would do. The Chairman of the Council died at the hands of the IRA and I'm still here preaching the Gospel and there is a Church in Armagh today.

I could give you the lifestory of twenty prominent personalities in Ulster Chiefs of Police, business men, religious leaders and they died in very strange circumstances. Every one of them hated and detested and worked against the Free Presbyterian Church. You say to me, 'How did you get your ground in the end?' I lifted my eyes to the hills. There was a lovely site on one of the hills of Armagh. I said to a fellow, 'Who owns that?' He said, 'It is a Brethren man.' I said, 'I am glad it is not an Irish Presbyterian, now there is hope for us.' He said, 'If you gathered up a thousand pounds and you offered it to him for the ground, you could get it.'

It is a site worth over a hundred thousand pounds today. I gathered up a thousand pounds, do not ask me how! There are men in this hall today and I could look them in the eye, I used to go and knock on their doors and say, 'I could do with a hundred pounds.' 'You will get it.' 'I could do with £500.' 'You will get it.' I went down with the money in my pocket. I went to his place of business and said, 'I want that ground of yours.' He said, 'Have you a thousand notes? It must be in cash.' I said, 'I have it here.' He said, 'We will do business.' He gave me the name of his solicitor and he took the money and I bought that ground which Brother Cooke occupies 'till Jesus comes or he gets a call to a bigger congregation!

I could go on and on. I recall a Roman Catholic police officer, a Head Constable who loved to take his stick and beat up the Free Presbyterians as they protested. One day he was cursing us in Donegal Pass station and one of the fellow constables said, 'I would not curse those people, something could happen to you.' He laughed and in a moment he choked and fell down behind the counter and he was in God's eternity. He was meeting the God he defied.

I remember a business man who was sitting in a plush office behind his desk cursing me. There was a fellow in front of him and he said, 'I would not curse that man.' Suddenly he choked and died in that very office.

John Wylie and I had an opponent in Ballymoney. He built an amazing new structure on his farm, a very sophisticated barn and it was the talk of the countryside. Everybody went to see it. He stood up in that barn and cursed Wylie and Paisley to the lowest hell. There was a man there who said to him, 'I would not do that, their God could come some night and lift your barn and twist every bit of iron in it and put it on the other side of the road.' The man laughed and said, 'You are a fool.' God sent a wind a few hours later and lifted that barn and twisted every girder in it and He put it on the other side of the road. Just to add insult to injury John Wylie went down to look over God's handiwork. He said, 'Lord you did it well. I could not have improved on it.'

If we come to the Lord, in unity with the Lord, nothing can stop us. You go out tomorrow morning with a teaspoon and try to stop the Lagan. You will work all day but it will still be flowing at teatime. You can't stop this Church if God is in it.

Take the blessing of God out of this Church and it will fold and fade away. But give us God's blessing and we will be mighty to the pulling down of strongholds of the Devil. We are in a better position to work for God today than we ever were. We have buildings, we have properties, we have ministers, we have a training college, we are working in four continents of the world and we have got to get into the fifth continent. God wants us to move forward, but you have to first pass the examination. I say, 'Oh God help me to pass the examination.'

THREE - THE ENGAGEMENT TO BE EFFECTED

Notice four things about these men. **First they had an affinity with David.** They were knit with David. Oh to be knit to the Lord Jesus Christ, to be as close to Jesus as it is possible to be. I want to profess to you, friend, with all my heart,

I love Jesus Christ. I love Him. I am not worthy of His love, but I love Him with all my heart, with all my soul and with all my mind. I grieve over my sins, I grieve over my failures, but I love the Lord. These men had an affinity with David.

Secondly, they had loyalty to David. They said, 'Thine are we, David, and on thy side.' There is no use saying, 'God bless the Free Presbyterian Church' and then stay in apostasy. You have got to shout out, get out and stay out. If every Christian left the ecumenical churches in Ulster we would have a revival tomorrow.

How can you stay in a church that is associated with praying to the spirits of the dead? It is more than I can understand. Read what happened at the WCC Assembly in Canberra, Australia. Lesbianism, homosexuality held up as taught in the Bible and to be practised by Christian people, think of it! Praying for the dead. They are even praying to the rain forests of Brazil. Think of it! They are praying to the jelly baby spirits caught in nuclear fall out. Think of it!

I feel like old Elijah, he mocked the god of Baal and I would mock these gods of the World Council of Churches. They be no gods. There is only One True and Living God and that is the Lord Jesus.

I am loyal to Jesus in religion, I am loyal to Jesus in politics, I am loyal to Jesus in morals. I am on the side of Christ in these issues. I want to emphasise that.

Thirdly, they had unity in David. 'Peace, peace be to thee and to thy helpers.'

Fourthly, they had spirituality along with David. You know why he said this? He said it because the Spirit of God came upon him. May the Spirit of God come upon us today! Seek my brother, my sister, to be filled with the Holy Spirit.

As I finish this great Conventicle that God has given me the privilege of addressing, I say, O, blessed Jesus, we salute Thee again. We hail Thee again. We honour Thee again. Thou art God of gods, Light of lights, Very God of Very God and Very Man of Very Man. We salute Thee because of the Glory that Thou hadst with the Father before all worlds.

In the Father's bosom the Shekinah Glory rested upon Thee, and all the angels of God worshipped Thee. We honour Thee because Thou didst humble Thyself and robed Thyself in robes of humanity and came down among the sons of men to identify everlastingly with human flesh and to become our elder brother for ever and to marry Thyself to Thy people. We salute Thee because on a Cross of wood - an old tree on the top of the hill of reproach - stark naked Thou didst hang, scoffed, spat upon, beaten, battered, broken, bleeding and Thou didst die for me.

Lord Jesus I honour Thee, I worship Thee, I love Thee, I praise Thee. If ever I loved Thee my Jesus 'tis now. Lord Jesus I go to Thy tomb but Thou art not there, Thou art gone for Thou art risen from the dead. Thou art no dying Christ on a crucifix. Thou art no dead Christ in a sepulchre. Thou art the Living Christ. Thou art alive for evermore and from Thy girdle dangle the keys of Hell and Death. Thou art Master of Heaven and Master of Hell. I salute Thee today because Thou art Risen, Ascended and at this very moment Thou art praying for me. But I salute Thee today because Thou art coming again.

Jesus Christ, brethren, is coming again. He has a word for you, 'Occupy till I come.' The best way to occupy is for every one of our members here today to say within their hearts, 'Thine are we, David, and on thy side, thou son of Jesse. Thine are we, Lord Jesus, and on Thy side, Thou Son of God.' I am asking you to bow your head now and close your eyes and in the secret of your heart to do business with God right now. I just want you, Christian to do one thing, I just want you to whisper, 'Thine are we, Lord Jesus, and on Thy side, Thou Son of God.' Will you do that? Do it now!

If there is a man or woman in this House unsaved, unforgiven, unpardoned, I wonder, today, will you cross over the line and say from today onward, 'I'm going to be on the side of the Lord Jesus. I am taking Him now as my Saviour and my Lord.'

CLOSING PRAYER

O God seal today the preaching of this message. Lord, may every believer, every preacher here, every minister here, every elder here, every communicant member here, every Sabbath School teacher here and scholar here who are Christ's, rededicate themselves to the cause of the Gospel. And, Lord, if there are sinners amongst us, bring them to Christ. Help them right now in that seat to call upon the Name of the Lord, for whosoever shall call upon the Name of the Lord shall be saved.'

Amen and Amen

12 The Queen's *Silver Jubilee*

A SERMON PREACHED IN 1977 IN THE MARTYRS MEMORIAL CHURCH ON THE OCCASION OF THE QUEEN'S SILVER JUBILEE. THE TEXT WAS PROVERBS 8:15 "BY ME KINGS REIGN, AND PRINCES DECREE JUSTICE." A SPECIALLY PRINTED COPY OF THIS SERMON WAS SENT TO THE QUEEN.

TURN TO PROVERBS CHAPTER eight and verse fifteen: "By me kings reign, and princes decree justice."

In this Silver Jubilee Year we say solemnly, sincerely, and joyfully, "God save the Queen!" When I say that I say it, first of all, in **supplication**, because the Queen needs to have a personal experience of God's salvation. We should all pray continually that our Monarch comes to know Jesus Christ and becomes a truly redeemed, regenerate child of God.

Secondly, it is a national prayer, because in praying for the salvation of the Queen we are praying for a national deliverance from everything that brings dishonour and that brings God's curse upon us as a nation.

We, of course, use the expression "God save the Queen" in a tone of **jubilation**, because we rejoice in the years that God has graciously given to our Monarch. We thank God for the preservation and for the sustenance that God has been to her, and to the Royal House of Windsor.

There is also a note of **anticipation**. I do not believe that God is finished with our nation. I believe that God has a purpose, that God has a plan and that God has a programme for Britain. I am confident that God has a purpose, and that God has a plan, and that God has a programme for Ulster. It could be that in this little part of Ireland oppressed by many enemies, maligned across the world by false, evil and black propaganda, that here as in the day of the Williamite Revolution, the battle will be fought and won to preserve our Protestant way of life.

Having made those preliminary remarks, could I say there are four things which we need to consider at this time of Her Majesty's Jubilee.

The first thing is the **Claim of the Monarch's Right.**

The second thing is the **Character of the Monarch's Royalty.**

The third thing is the **Commitment of the Monarch's Realm.**

The last thing is the **Consequence of the Monarch's Reign.**

I want to consider these four things with you.

But let me first say from this pulpit that our highest allegiance, that our first sworn submission is not to any earthly Monarch, is not to the House of Windsor, is not to Her Majesty, Queen Elizabeth the Second, that our first, our highest, our greatest loyalty is to the KING OF KINGS AND LORD OF LORDS. Our second loyalty to any earthly Monarch is only as it is compatible with our first loyalty to the Lord Jesus Christ.

We are descendants and proud to be descendants of the Scottish Covenanters. With them we can say, "Christ alone reigns as Christ alone saves."

I am reminded of a charge made against certain people who believe that there was another King, even Jesus. It was a charge made against the apostles. Mark it in your Bible. It is an important text. Acts chapter seventeen and verse seven, *"these all do contrary to the decrees of Caesar, saying that there is another King, one Jesus."* Hallelujah! Another King. He is our King, and He is KING OF KINGS, and He is LORD OF LORDS.

I am also reminded of the old Covenanting preacher, Alexander Melville, who when he was talking to King James VI of Scotland, afterwards James I of England, said, "Your Majesty, there are two kings and two kingdoms in this realm of Scotland. There is the Kingdom of Scotland of which you are King, and of which I am a subject. But there is also the Kingdom of Jesus Christ. And you, your Majesty, are no King in that Kingdom. You are also a subject in that Kingdom. And the KING of that Kingdom is One Jesus Christ, the sole KING and only Head of the Church."

That is our principle too. When the laws of this nation are contrary to the laws of King Jesus, we know where our loyalty lies. We know what line of action we will be pursuing, Let no one have any doubts about that particular matter.

I. THE CLAIMS OF THE MONARCH'S RIGHT

Queen Elizabeth has **a birthright** to the British Throne. As a result of birth she has a right to ascend the Throne of England, the Throne of the United Kingdom and the dominions. It is based upon birth.

I turn to the KING OF KINGS AND LORD OF LORDS. I think of the first question which is asked in the Old Testament. The first question asked in the Old Testament was asked by God. It was asked concerning man. God said, "Where art thou?" But the first question asked in the New Testament was a question of man concerning God, and it was, "Where is He that is born King of the Jews?" The wondrous Birth of the KING OF KINGS AND LORD OF LORDS.

In the pedigree of our Sovereign there are those that bring a stain upon the history book, that left behind them evil deeds, evil speeches and evil things. But who can question the pedigree of Him who was born of a pure Virgin, and who is perfect Man, impeccable Humanity in which God Himself is Incarnate and in which Deity itself is enthroned.

Of course the Queen has **a legal right** to the Throne. And, of course, that legal right is founded upon her declaration at the Coronation, "I am a faithful Protestant." If tomorrow the Royal House of Windsor became Roman Catholic, and if tomorrow her successor became a Roman Catholic, then I would have no allegiance whatsoever to the British Throne or to the House of Windsor. That is not a very popular thing to say, but that is the Constitution of this land. Let us make it clear that the Queen has a right to reign only if she is a faithful Protestant, only if she has no relationship or agreement with the Vatican, only as she keeps to the Williamite Revolution Settlement.

Of course there is a great attack upon that today. There was a deplorable article this week in the "Belfast Telegraph" against those that would protest against a Massing priest at the central service to commemorate Her Majesty's Jubilee. Who gave the Irish Presbyterian Church the authority to have the official service? I do not know. Or who gave the Archbishop of Armagh the right to say that he was the official preacher of an official service? There is no State Church in this land, nor an established Church in this part of the Queen's dominions. These Ecumenists arrogated to themselves a right that is not theirs. They took upon them an authority that is not theirs and could never be theirs. But there were those inside the Irish Presbyterian Church, a small remnant, nevertheless they voiced grave disapproval at this action. The "Belfast Telegraph" issues a scurrilous attack upon them. It says that they have no right to make this sort of protest. This, they say, is against Christianity.

I want to say the honour of Jesus Christ is more important to me than the honour of the Queen. I want to say from this pulpit that a Massing priest at that service is an insult to God Almighty, and the Sacrifice which the Lord Jesus offered upon the Cross.

If it is true (And one does not know whether to believe Jack Weir or not, for he has said so many things that one doubts his veracity and integrity), what he says, that the Queen, at Holyrood Palace, expressed delight that a Roman Priest should be at her Jubilee service, and no sorrow at IRA atrocities, then it is sad indeed.

I see Jack Weir was holding forth against Mr Mason and his disastrous security policies. But let us not forget that the same gentleman was down at the Feakle talks negotiating with the IRA gunmen and seeking to get a settlement in favour of Republicanism.

Is it not amazing also that the Archbishop of Armagh should be the preacher at that service when on the 50th Anniversary of the Rebellion of 1916 he had a special service in the Cathedral in Dublin to thank God for the successful and bloody rebellion against the British Crown and the British Parliament?

Here we have a two-faced clergyman. When he was in Dublin he celebrated rebellion against the Crown. When he comes North he celebrates the Jubilee of Her Majesty.

I want to say from this pulpit, as dogmatically as I can, we know to Whom our final allegiance is. And if there should be any rejection by the House of Windsor of the Coronation Oath, then, as far as I am concerned, my allegiance to the House of Windsor will no longer be obligatory.

These are truths which need to be spelt out and spelt out with great plainness. Unless you go into the quagmire of Ecumenism today you will be labelled as a bigoted extremist, a person who should have lived in the 16th Century, a person who has not forgotten the controversies of the 17th Century!

I was telling a critic of mine the other day, "I am sorry you do not put me far enough back in history. I go back to the first century for my Christianity and for my creed."

II. THE CHARACTER OF THE MONARCH'S ROYALTY

Let me come to the character of the Monarch's Royalty. The character of the Monarch is important. Some of the kings and queens of England were wicked people, people who were ruled by their own vices, their blasphemies, and their immoralities which brought a curse upon the Realm.

We know what happened to Charles I, how the Parliament and people of England had to convict him of being an evil murderer. They had to carry out the act of capital punishment upon his person, and rid the land of a tyrant and of a monster. My sympathies are wholly with Oliver Cromwell and wholly with the Parliamentary struggle against tyranny and arbitrary power in that epoch of our history.

We also know what the people of these islands had to do with the other Stuart Monarch, James the Second. How he had to be driven from this land. William, Prince of Orange, had to be brought from Holland to take the Throne to re-establish Protestant truth, to reassert Protestant liberty from arbitrary power in these lands.

We thank God for a good Queen. We thank God for her example as a wife. We thank God for her example as a mother. We thank God for her example as a Constitutional Monarch. I am sure we were all delighted at what she said, when she addressed the Houses of Parliament recently, and received their address of loyalty, "I remember I was crowned Queen of the United Kingdom; England, Wales, Scotland and Northern Ireland." That brought satisfaction to us all. We thank God for the person of the Queen. We deeply regret the insidious influence of Ecumenism in the Royal House. We regret that the Monarch has, from time to time, been guilty of shameful desecration of the Lord's Day, and by giving an example to her citizens and her subjects, has turned the Lord's Day, a Holy Day, into a holiday. We mourn that fact. We have protested against it, and will continue to protest against it. But we thank God for all the gracious qualities of our Gracious Sovereign Lady.

I turn now to the character of the KING OF KINGS. We have never seen during our time upon this earth perfect humanity, but He is Perfect Humanity.

No valid criticism can be made against the Saviour. No hand can be pointed against the Immaculate Person of God manifest in flesh. He is Holy, Harmless, Undefiled, Separate from sinners, the Sinless, Spotless, Harmless, Crimeless, Son of God. To the Character of His Eternal Royalty we bow in wonderment and amazement and we worship.

III. THE COMMITMENT OF THE MONARCH'S REALM

Could I say a brief word about the Commitment of the Monarch's Realm.

Each one of us has a commitment to Queen Elizabeth the Second. This commitment came to us by our birth as subjects of the House of Windsor.

Could I draw a parallel? You will never be loyal to King Jesus except you are born again. It is in the new birth, in the mystery, in the secret, in the supernaturalness of the new birth that my loyalty to Christ originates and my loyalty to Christ is established.

How many people here are trusting in themselves, trusting in the Church, trusting in their baptism, trusting in the Lord's Supper, trusting in Protestant loyalty, trusting in the things good in their proper place, but not trusting only and forever in the Blood of Christ?

Further, our loyalty to the Queen is a personal loyalty which we have publicly professed. Each one of us, as we have sung the National Anthem together, has made a personal commitment to the Queen.

The Bible tells me that if I believe in my heart and confess with my mouth that Jesus Christ is Lord, that He is King, I shall be saved.

Tell me today, have you made that public committal of yourself to the KING OF KINGS AND LORD OF LORDS?

IV. THE CONSEQUENCE OF THE MONARCH'S REIGN

A final word about the Consequence of the Monarch's reign.

The Queen has given stability in an unstable day to our land. The institution of the Monarchy is an institution that has stood the test of time. The rising tides of Republicanism have failed to really corrode this important rock of the Constitutional Monarchy of our land. The Monarchy provides continuity. Parliaments go. Thank God they do! Prime Ministers go. Thank God they do! But the Queen goes on. And when one Monarch dies another Monarch automatically takes his or her place, and the Queen and King live on. And in the Monarchy there is the continuance of the Kingdom.

Thank God there is a KING Whose Dominion shall never end. There is One Who is crowned KING. Truly of Him it can be said, O King live forever.

"Crowns and Thrones may perish,
Kingdoms rise and fall,"

But God's KING shall reign for evermore. There is no end to the Kingdom of Jesus. He never grows old in the exercise of His Royal prerogatives. His power to pardon is as strong today as it was when He pardoned Adam and Eve at the beginning of the history of mankind. The Throne of God shall stand for evermore, and will have perpetual and eternal victory. Yes, and one day the kingdoms of this world shall become the kingdoms of our Lord and of His Christ, and He shall reign. And we, by grace, through faith shall reign with Him.

May God bless these words and let us keep in mind the declaration of a Sovereign God, "By me kings reign, and princes decree justice."

Amen and Amen

13 There's no place *like Hell!*

A SERMON PREACHED IN 1988 IN THE MARTYRS MEMORIAL CHURCH ON THE OCCASION OF THE RESURGENCE OF THE "NO HELL THEOLOGY" AMONGST SO-CALLED EVANGELICALS. THE TEXT WAS LUKE 16:24 "AND IN HELL HE LIFT UP HIS EYES."

ON AN AMERICAN TROOPSHIP during World War II a new Chaplain came aboard. The rank and file of the sailors met him and they put to him this question, *"Do you believe in Hell?"* The Chaplain was a modernist and an unbeliever, and he said, *"Men, certainly not."* The men looked at him and said, *"Sir, we would like you to resign as Chaplain of this troopship. If there is no Hell we do not require your services, but if there is a Hell we are not going to be deceived by the like of you."*

Those sailors were speaking solemn truth. If there is no Hell, then there is no need for you to come to the House of God, there is no need for you to read the Bible, there is no need for you to be concerned about your soul's Eternity.

But if there is a Hell then you need to ask yourself one solemn question, *"Is that where I am going to be forever? How can I escape from its worm which never dieth, and its fire which is never quenched?"*

FIVE LIES ABOUT HELL

In Luke's Gospel chapter sixteen, I want you to notice how in a few short sentences the Lord Jesus Christ demolished the devil's lies and man's falsehoods concerning Hell.

The **first** great lie and the first great falsehood that the devil propagates and man accepts is this, that *Hell is what you make of life down here*. Hell is in this life. The Lord Jesus demolished that lie, for He said, (and look carefully at it,) *"The rich man"* verse 22, *"also died and was buried, and in Hell he lifted up his eyes.."* So Hell is not what you make in this life. It is the after-life.

The **second** lie of the devil and the second falsehood that men embrace is, *"Hell is annihilation. When you die that is the finish."*

I remember hearing the late Lord Brookeborough interviewed about his beliefs, and he said, "When I die that is the end." What a fool he was! When he died he unlearned that lie very speedily in Eternity. God says in His Book that *After death in Hell the rich man lifted up his eyes, being in torments.* Hell is not annihilation.

The **third** lie of the devil and the third falsehood men embrace is, *"Hell is soul-sleep in absolute unconsciousness."*

The Lord Jesus Christ demolished that lie as well, for He shewed the consciousness of the rich man in Hell. He said he was in torments. He was totally and absolutely conscious.

The **fourth** lie of the devil and the fifth falsehood believed by men is, *"Hell is a purgatory that fits the soul for Heaven."*

The Lord Jesus demolished that lie. He said that between Heaven and Hell there is a great gulf fixed, and no one ever passed from Hell to Heaven.

The unbridgeable gulf between Heaven and Hell! So Hell is not a purgatory from which sin is cleansed from the soul, and the soul is prepared for Heaven.

The **fifth** lie of the devil and the fifth falsehood believed by man is, *"Hell is a place where departed souls can communicate with their loved ones on earth."*

In the rising tide of demonism and witchcraft today we are told by so-called spiritualists, who are not spiritual at all but are spiritists, that the dead can communicate with the living.

If this rich man could have communicated with his living brethren then he would not have asked Abraham to send Lazarus to talk to them.

The Lord demolished those five colossal lies propagated by the devil and accepted by men, and those five lies form the basis of all anti-Hell theology and the beliefs of all those who oppose the plain teaching of the Bible about the doctrine of Hell.

THERE'S NO PLACE LIKE HELL ... FOR THERE IS NO DARKNESS LIKE THE DARKNESS OF HELL

Firstly, there is no place like Hell, for there is no darkness like the darkness of Hell. Hear it, there is no place like Hell, for there is no darkness like the darkness of Hell.

The Lord Jesus Christ issued three solemn warnings about the darkness of Hell.

He spoke, first of all, in Matthew 8:12 and said, *"But the children of the kingdom shall be cast out into outer darkness."* Notice the words, "outer darkness". In Matthew 22:13 he said, *"Bind him hand and foot, and take him away and cast him into outer darkness."* In Matthew 25:30 He said, *"Cast the unprofitable servant into outer darkness."*

It is darkness which is completely beyond any ray of light. Outer darkness! It is outside all light, all natural light, all man-made light, all spiritual light, all God-given light, all the light of the gospel, all the light of hope, all the light of peace and all the light of pardon. It is outer darkness. It is outside all light.

In Jude verse 13 we read of the *"blackness of darkness forever"*. That is where the ungodly go. Not only into outer darkness but into the blackness of darkness forever.

As I sat in my study I thought of the darkness into which my readers would most certainly go if they died outside Jesus Christ. I said to myself, *"Did the shadow of that darkness ever fall upon this world? Did ever the darkness of Hell overshadow this world?"*

As the darkness of Hell is the result of God's inflexible and God's unchangeable and God's Holy judgment, I thought upon judgment days.

If you go back to a time of judgments in the Book of Exodus you will remember that one of the judgments in Egypt was darkness.

For three days, God decided to allow the darkness of Hell to rest upon Egypt. In the tenth chapter we read of that darkness, verse 21, *"And the Lord said unto Moses, Stretch out thine hand toward heaven that there may be darkness over the land of Egypt, even darkness which may be felt. And Moses stretched forth his hand toward heaven, and there was a thick darkness in all the land of Egypt three days. They saw not one another, neither rose any from his place for three days, but all the children of Israel had light in their dwellings."*

It was a darkness that could be felt. It was such a blanket of intense outer black darkness that they could see absolutely nothing. All they could do was lie in terror upon their beds for nothing could be seen. God permitted the darkness of Hell for three days to settle upon Egypt. Then I thought of that place called Calvary. I thought of that day when God judged His Well Beloved Son. Luke records it in his Gospel chapter 23 and verse 44, *"And it was about the sixth hour, and there was a darkness over all the earth until the ninth hour."*

The darkness of Hell into which Jesus went at Calvary, was so intense and widespread that it spread over all the world. There was not a country, there was not a village, there was not a people not overshadowed in that terrible darkness. It was a warning to the world and it was a warning to sinners that there is no darkness like the darkness of Hell, for there's no place like Hell.

Your unsaved soul will be cut off from light forever, never again to see anything. You will be in a blind darkness, wrapped up in the impenetrable folds of God's doom and damnation forever. There is no darkness like the darkness of Hell.

THERE IS NO PLACE LIKE HELL ... FOR THERE IS NO LONELINESS LIKE THE LONELINESS OF HELL

Secondly, there is no place like Hell for there is no loneliness like the loneliness of Hell. The lost soul, Christ says, will be bound hand and foot, and then cast into the outer darkness, the blackness of darkness in his lonely eternal prison cell forever.

Hell is a place of eternal isolation. Hell is a place of everlasting separation. Hell is a place of never ending unrelieved and unrelievable loneliness.

The fool laughs and says, *"Oh, I will have plenty of good company in Hell. All my sinful companions will be there. All the people I have lived in sin with and enjoyed the pleasures of earth with, preacher, will all be there. So I will have plenty of company in Hell."*

Friend, Hell does not want you, and Hell will not welcome you. There will be no reception committee of your old companions at Hell's gates to welcome you when you arrive in the place of the damned. Every damned soul is so tormented in the flames of Hell and in the agony of the torments of eternal doom, that he or she cannot spare a moment to think of others in Hell, to speak to others in Hell, or to communicate with others in Hell. Like in the darkness of Egypt the lost cannot see one solitary thing.

Every cell in Hell is built for eternal solitary confinement. Just think about that. The bars on the cell of Hell shut out all prisoners and the prisoner does his eternal sentence alone, alone, alone! The only thought for others which enters the mind, the memory and the heart of the damned is a cry for their loved one still on earth. Who did that damned rich man cry for? He cried for his brothers at home. He cried for his family. He cried for his relations that they would not come to this place of torment. He had not one word to speak of any who were already in Hell, for Hell is a place of loneliness.

We do not like to be alone. There are some things that cheer our hearts. There is nothing so happy as to take a little one upon your knees and hear the childish prattle and the childish talk. There are no children in Hell for you to talk to, for Hell is a place of loneliness. The only children in Hell are the children of the devil and the children of everlasting wrath.

When we want to tell someone we are thinking about them to cheer them in their loneliness, we send them flowers. Flowers are beautiful things. We live in a day of imitation. Men try to make flowers. Did you ever put a man-made rose beside the real thing? You take an imitation rose, anoint it with the scent or perfume of the rose and then take the real thing and smell the scent of that beautiful rose, and you will exclaim, *How poor and hopeless the imitation is!* The only flowers in Hell are the ashes of lost hope, lost joy and lost opportunities of Gospel pardon. The only flowers you will have in Hell, will be such ashes. There is loneliness in Hell.

There is nothing relieves loneliness like music. We all have our choices in music. To hear someone sing or to hear some particular instrument chases away loneliness and brings back thoughts of society and friends, and pleasantly stirs the memory. There is no music in Hell. The only thing you will hear in Hell will be the signs and the groans of damned souls. There is loneliness in Hell.

I like the mountains. I like the valleys. I like the rivers. I like the lakes and the seas and the oceans. The only mountains in Hell are mountains of everlasting flames. The only valleys in Hell are the troughs of the brimstone fire. The only lake is Hell itself for Hell is a lake of fire. The only sea in Hell is the sea of the everlasting burning. In Hell there is not one drop of water. It is a place of intense loneliness, and all they have to drink is the wine of God's wrath.

To that **Loneliness** unconverted one, you are most certainly headed. *"Knowing the terror of the Lord we persuade men,"* II Cor. 5:11.

THERE IS NO PLACE LIKE HELL ... FOR THERE IS NO RESTLESSNESS LIKE THE RESTLESSNESS OF HELL

Thirdly, there is no place like Hell, for there is no restlessness like the restlessness of Hell. Hell is a place of darkness, yes, of loneliness, yes, and of restlessness.

Revelation chapter 14 is a solemn word. It is the Word of the Living God. We read there in verses 10 and 11, *"The same shall drink of the wine of the wrath of God, which is poured out without mixture into the cup of his indignation, and he shall be tormented with fire and brimstone in the presence of the holy angels, and in the presence of the Lamb. And the smoke of their torment ascendeth up for ever and ever, and they have no rest day nor night."*

Young people do not appreciate what a wonderful thing it is to rest. Young people never want to go to bed, and then when they go to bed they never want to get up. They do not appreciate rest. But when you are busy, especially in the service of God, you thank God for the blessing of rest.

Jesus said to His hard worked disciples, *"Come ye apart and rest awhile." "He giveth His beloved sleep."*

Oh, how sweet is the rest of God! Heaven is described in the words, *"There remaineth, therefore, a rest for the people of God."*

The great Puritan Richard Baxter wrote about this and called it *"The Saints' Everlasting Rest."*

There is no rest in Hell. You know why there is no rest in Hell? Because Hell is the place of **Separation from God**, and the only place man can find rest is in God.

As David Brainerd rode the bridle trails of the forest seeking the Indians to whom God had called him to preach the Gospel, he used to cry as he rode his horse, *"There is no rest but in God."* What a message! Thank God there is rest in Him. Hell is the place of separation from God, and there cannot be any rest. The only Person that can give you rest is Christ. *"Come unto me all ye that labour and are heavy laden, and I will give you rest."* If you have not got rest in Christ, some day you will witness and experience the restlessness of Hell.

There is no rest in Hell because of the **Sin in Hell**, and sin breeds restlessness. Where sin is there is no peace. Where sin is there is no rest. Where sin is there cannot be any stillness. There cannot be any rest where sin is. Isaiah verses 20 and 21, *"But the wicked are like the troubled sea when it cannot rest, whose* *waters cast up mire and dirt, There is no peace,"* saith my God, *"to the wicked."* Over Hell God has said, *There is no peace to the wicked.*

There is no rest in Hell because of the **Shame of Hell**. In Revelation chapter 21 and verse 8 we read of the Shame of Hell. Hell is a shameful place, *"The fearful, the unbelieving, the abominable, murderers, whoremongers, sorcerers, idolaters and all liars shall have their part in the lake which burneth with fire and brimstone, which is the second death."*

There is no rest in Hell because of the **Sufferings of Hell**. You say to me, "Do you believe in literal fire in Hell?" Yes, I do! "Why do you believe that?" Because that is exactly what Jesus Christ taught, and He is the only One that knew and could tell us. In Matthew chapter 13, He told the story of the tares of the field and He gave the interpretation thereof.

He interpreted who the sower was and

What the field was, *"the field is the world".*

What the good seed were, *"the children of the kingdom".*

Who the tares were, *"the children of the wicked one."*

Who the enemy was, *"the enemy was the devil."*

When the harvest was, *"it is the end of the world."*

Who the reapers were, *"they were the angels."*

Then He said, *"As therefore the tares are gathered and burned in the fire, so shall it be in the end of the world."*

My friend, if that fire was not fire, Jesus was duty bound to have finished the interpretation and told us what it was. But there is fire in Hell, and forever, lost soul, you will be tormented in that flame. You ask, "How could there be darkness in Hell if there is a flame of fire?" The hottest flame known to man, scientifically, is a flame that is dark. How dark is that flame that will scourge lost souls and take away their rest in Hell.

THERE IS NO PLACE LIKE HELL ... FOR THERE IS NO ENDLESSNESS LIKE THE ENDLESSNESS OF HELL

We sing the hymn concerning grace,
> *"When we've been there ten thousand years,*
> *Bright shining as the sun,*
> *We've no less days to sing God' praise,*
> *Than when we first begun!"*

What is true of Heaven is true of Hell. When you have been in Hell ten trillion years in the darkness, the torments will have just begun. There is endlessness in Hell. It never ends.

If we could say to the damned, "After ten million, trillion years these doors will open, this burning and this darkness will give place to light, this loneliness to society, this endlessness will have its end," then hope would spring eternal even in the breast of the damned. But there is no such thing as this torment having an end.

Every century there is always controversy about Hell. In the last century the controversy was in Scotland about the doctrine of Hell. At that time there was a great scholar and a great Evangelical minister called Dr James Morison. He said, "I'm going to find out, I'm going to find out if there is any hope for a soul who goes to Hell." He made a thorough study from Matthew to Revelation, and one day he got up and closed his Greek Testament, and said, "There is no hope, for Hell has no ending."

The saddest road to Hell is to pass by the Word of God. The saddest road to Hell is to close your ears to the warning of the blessed Holy Spirit, your eyes to the Son of God, and pass from the Gospel message to the blackness of darkness forever.

It will be more tolerable in the day of judgment for Sodom and Gomorrah than it will be for a man or a woman who reads this Gospel tract and said, "NO" to Jesus Christ.

These are my final words to you, and I say to you, as we gaze out into the darkness of Hell, into the loneliness of Hell, into the restlessness of Hell, and into the endlessness of Hell, *"Make haste to Calvary, wash in the Saviour's Blood, come this night to the Saviour and in God's Name be in time."*

Amen and Amen

14 Back to *the Cross*

A SERMON PREACHED ON LORD'S DAY MORNING 11TH OCTOBER, 1987 IN THE MARTYRS MEMORIAL CHURCH AND BROADCAST ON BBC RADIO ULSTER AND RADIO 4. THE TEXT WAS I CORINTHIANS 1:17-18,23-24 "FOR CHRIST SENT ME NOT TO BAPTISE BUT TO PREACH THE GOSPEL; NOT WITH THE WISDOM OF WORDS, LEST THE CROSS OF CHRIST SHOULD BE MADE OF NONE EFFECT. FOR THE PREACHING OF THE CROSS IS TO THEM THAT PERISH FOOLISHNESS; BUT UNTO US WHICH ARE SAVED IT IS THE POWER OF GOD. BUT WE PREACH CHRIST CRUCIFIED, UNTO THE JEWS A STUMBLING BLOCK, AND UNTO THE GREEKS FOOLISHNESS; BUT UNTO THEM WHO ARE CALLED, BOTH JEW AND GREEKS, CHRIST THE POWER OF GOD, AND THE WISDOM OF GOD."

ORGANISED 20th CENTURY CHURCHIANITY has lost the power, the drive, the influence and the motivation of unorganised 1st century Christianity.

It is simply a question of basics.

20th century churchianity is in the sacramental business, 1st century Christianity was in the salvation business.

20th century churchianity is in the inoffensive business, 1st century Christianity was in the offensive business.

20th century churchianity was in the denominational business, 1st century Christianity was in the divine business.

20th century churchianity is in the ecumenical business, 1st century Christianity was in the evangelistic business.

20th century churchianity is in the roaming business, 1st century Christianity was in the redeeming business.

Thus real progress has been halted.

Treason overshadows truth, hypocrisy overshadows holiness, penance overshadows penitence and purgatory overshadows paradise.

Anaemic churchianity needs a blood transfusion. We all need to get to the blood bank of Calvary. We need to return to a Bible based, Christ centred, Cross dominated Christianity.

Paul gives us the answer to the secret of the success of 1st century Christianity and the remedy for the situation which has developed today.

His words are plain, uncompromising and crystal clear, I Corinthians 1:17, 18, 23, 24.

"For Christ sent me not to baptise but to preach the Gospel; not with the wisdom of words, lest the Cross of Christ should be made of none effect. For the preaching of the Cross is to them that perish foolishness; but unto us which are saved it is the Power of God. But we preach Christ Crucified, unto the Jews a stumbling block, and unto the Greeks foolishness; but unto them who are called, both Jew and Greeks, Christ the Power of God, and the Wisdom of God."

First our attention is called to:

I. THE CROSS - DEFINED

Some have claimed that they possess actual pieces of the true Cross. It is a fact that if all these pieces were brought together there would be enough wood to make a multiplicity of crosses! But what of it.

Paul makes it crystal clear that it is not the wood of the Cross which saves but the work done on the Cross by our Lord Jesus Christ.

The only actual definitive description of the death gallows of the Son of God in the New Testament is "a tree"; "The God of our fathers raised up Jesus, whom he slew and hanged on a *tree*." Acts 5:30.

"Who His Own Self bare our sins in His Own Body on *the tree*, that we, being dead to sins, should live unto righteousness: by whose stripes ye are healed." I Peter 2:24.

Note it carefully. Paul declares, "The preaching of the Cross is to them that perish foolishness but to us who are saved it is the Power of God." And then he defines what that Cross is and what its preaching is. He states, "We preach Christ crucified." It is not the material of the Cross, it is the making of the atonement at the at-one-ment on the Cross which is the Cross as defined and declared by the Apostle.

The Cross then is that final, all sufficient, never to be repeated, saving sacrifice of Christ on the accursed tree, whereby through the shedding of His most precious Blood the Lord Jesus Christ accomplished Salvation for all those who put their trust in Him.

That is the only Cross Paul knows. That is the only Cross Paul proclaims. That is the only Cross Paul glories in. He defines his preaching thus:

"Moreover, brethren, I declare unto you the Gospel which I preached unto you, which also ye have received, and in which ye stand: by which also ye are saved, if ye keep in memory what I preached unto you, unless ye have believed in vain.

"For I delivered unto you first of all that which I also received that Christ died for our sins according to the Scriptures; and that He was buried, and that He rose again the third day according to the Scriptures; and that He was seen of Cephas, then of the twelve." I Corinthians 15:1-5.

The Cross - defined.

Secondly our attention is called to:

II. THE CROSS - DISTINCT

Paul proclaimed that Christ sent him not to baptise but to preach the Gospel. He is not commissioned by Christ to administer sacraments. He is commissioned to announce the Sacrifice of the Cross. He is not a priest, he is a preacher. The Cross is distinct. It stands alone. It tolerates no rivals in the saving message of the Gospel. It is eternally unique.

The centrality of the Cross is the great recurring theme of Paul's ministry. "Christ sent me not to baptise," he thunders, "but to preach the Gospel." "I thank God that I baptise none of you."

The application of baptismal water does not save the soul, only the application of the Blood of Christ can work salvation in the heart of sinners.

Yes, the Cross is distinct.

It is the Sacrifice which ended all sacrifices. Hear the Word of the Lord. "And every priest standeth daily ministering and offering oftentimes the same sacrifices which can never take away sins. But this Man, after He had offered one Sacrifice for sins forever sat down on the Right Hand of God. From henceforth expecting till His enemies be made His footstool. For by one offering He hath perfected for ever them that are the sanctified." Hebrews 10:11-14.

The Cross - distinct.
Thirdly our attention is called to:

III. THE CROSS - DECLARED

The only Divinely appointed way for the setting forth of the Cross is by preaching - making announcement - declaring from a throne - heralding the message.

"For it is written I will destroy the wisdom of the wise and will bring to nothing the understanding of the prudent.

"Where is the wise? Where is the Scribe? Where is the disputer of this world? Hath not God made foolish the wisdom of this world? For after that, in the wisdom of God, the world by wisdom knew not God, it pleased God by the foolishness of preaching to save them that believe." I Corinthians 1:19-21.

The preaching has to be plain and rugged without ornament and additions.

"My speech," says Paul, "and my preaching was not with the enticing words of man's wisdom but in the demonstration of the spirit and of power." I Corinthians 2:4.

"We use," he says, "great plainness of speech." II Corinthians 3:12.

Yes, we are all sinners, "All have sinned and come short of the glory of God."

Sin is lawlessness. A violation of God's commands. God's law is summarised in the Ten Commandments. Listen to them:

"And God spoke all these words, saying, I am the Lord Thy God, Who have brought thee out of the land of Egypt, out of the house of bondage.

"1st, Thou shalt have no other gods before Me.

"2nd, Thou shalt not make unto thee any graven image, or any likeness of anything that is in heaven above, or earth beneath, or that is in the water under the earth; thou shalt not bow down thyself to them, nor serve them; for I, the Lord Thy God, am a jealous God, visiting the iniquity of the fathers upon the children unto the third and fourth generation of them that hate me; and showing mercy unto thousands of them that love Me and keep My Commandments.

"3rd, Thou shalt not take the name of the Lord thy God in vain; for the Lord will not hold him guiltless that taketh His Name in vain.

"4th, Remember the Sabbath Day to keep it Holy. Six days shalt thou labour and do all thy work; but on the seventh day is the Sabbath of the Lord thy

God; in it thou shalt not do any work, thou, nor thy son, nor thy daughter, nor thy manservant, nor thy maidservant, nor thy cattle, nor thy stranger that is within thy gates; for in six days the Lord made heaven and earth, the sea and all that in them is, and rested the seventh day: wherefore the Lord blessed the Sabbath Day and hallowed it.

"5th, Honour thy father and thy mother, that thy days may be long upon the land which the Lord thy God giveth thee.

"6th, Thou shalt not kill.

"7th, Thou shalt not commit adultery.

"8th, Thou shalt not steal.

"9th, Thou shalt not bear false witness against thy neighbour.

"10th, Thou shalt not covet thy neighbour's house; thou shalt not covet thy neighbour's wife, nor his manservant, nor his maidservant, nor his ox, nor his ass, nor anything that is thy neighbour's." Exodus 20:1-17.

The Lord Jesus stated that the law could be summed up thus: "Thou shalt love the Lord thy God with all thy heart, and with all thy soul, and with all thy mind. This is the first and great Commandment. And the second is like unto it, thou shalt love thy neighbour as thyself. On these two Commandments hang all the law and the prophets." Matt. 22:37-40.

You and I have violated these Commandments. You and I have not loved God with all our hearts.

If we are guilty of one violation we are guilty of all.

Sin is the transgression of the law.

Every sin deserves the curse of God and His wrath in hell forever. Christ has made Himself accountable in law, for the sins of His people.

God in His Sovereign Grace has devised means whereby His banished are not always expelled from Him. A transfer has taken place. Christ has taken responsibility to discharge the debt of our sin. God has made Him to be sin for us who knew no sin that we might be made the righteousness of God in Him. (II Cor. 5:21)

The Cross is a penal sacrifice, the penalty of my sin was endured by my substitute and my Saviour.

"But he was wounded for our transgressions, He was bruised for our iniquities: the chastisement of our peace was upon Him, and with His stripes we are healed." Isaiah 53:5.

The Cross in an "instead of me" sacrifice. Stroke for stroke, lash for lash, curse for curse, blow for blow, pang for pang, the Lord Jesus Christ born for me. With one tremendous draught He drank damnation dry for me.

Oh why was He there as the bearer of sin
If on Jesus my guilt was not laid,
Oh why from His side flowed the sin cleansing blood
If by dying my debt was not paid.

Look, look, look, and live!
There is life for a look at the Crucified One,
There is life at this moment for thee.

Then look sinner look unto
Him and be saved, unto
Him Who has died on the tree.

"Neither is there Salvation in any other; for there is none other name under Heaven given among men, whereby we must be saved." Acts 4:12.

The Cross - declared.

Fourthly our attention is called to:

IV. THE CROSS - DESPISED

The offence of the Cross has not ceased. Its message of the exceeding sinfulness of man's sin; its message of the necessity of blood atonement; its message of substitution; its message that every sin must receive eternal hell is repugnant to man's proud heart.

Proud 20th century man looks at himself as a giant and views God as a dwarf. He views himself as some superior being capable of judging the Almighty.

It was such pride that dug hell and damned the devil and it has been damning the devil's dupes ever since.

Proud sinner it is only through this Cross which you have despised that you can be saved. There is no other way. This is the only path to Heaven. The only key which can unlock Heaven's door. The only instrument which can bring about sin's pardon in your heart.

What folly is in the heart of sinners to seek to add to the cross. Men make it an ornament. A cross, an ornament, they will wear - but the true Cross, the atonement, they will not wear. Men will make it a relic, a cross a relic they will reverence - but the true Cross, the reconciliation, they will not receive. Men make it a sign, a cross, a sign, they will delight in - but the true Cross, the only sacrifice for sin, they discard. Men make it a memento, a cross, a memento, they defend - the true Cross, the miracle, they debase.

Add nothing to the Cross. Neither your works, your knowledge, your virtues, your religion, your churchmanship or your righteousness. Remember that open sin has killed its thousands but self righteousness its tens of thousands.

Despise not the Cross. Reject not its message. Become not its enemy. "Whosoever shall fall on this stone shall be broken (that is for deliverance) but on whomsoever it shall fall it will grind him to powder (that is for destruction)." Matt. 31:24.

The Cross - despised.

Lastly our attention is called to:

V. THE CROSS - DYNAMIC

The preaching of the Cross - the Power of God.

We preach Christ Crucified - Christ the Power of God and the Wisdom of God.

In this message of Christ dying for our sins according to the Scriptures, Christ being buried and Christ rising the third day according to the Scriptures, is the Almighty Power of Almighty God.

"A living Saviour dying, that a dying sinner might live", is the cream and essence, the pith and marrow of the whole Gospel.

You need grace - the Cross is the glorious fountain of grace. You need forgiveness - the Cross is the gracious bank of forgiveness.

You need hope - the Cross is the great anchor of hope. You need power - the Cross is the grand generator of power. You need a way to Heaven - the Cross is the gigantic ladder to Heaven.

The Cross not its signs but its sacrifice, the Cross not its emblem but its expiation, the Cross not its structure but its salvation, the Cross not its wood but its work, must be your whole trust and stay.

> *Stretched on the Cross, the Saviour dies,*
> *Hark! His expiring groans arise!*
> *See from His hands, His feet, His side,*
> *Runs down the sacred crimson tide!*
> *But life attends the deathful sound,*
> *And flows from every bleeding wound;*
> *The vital stream, how free it flows,*
> *To save and cleanse His rebel foes!*

Give yourself no rest till your heart beats in unison with Heaven. Turn from your sin, come to the Cross, wash in the precious Blood of Christ. Listen and lay hold of this sweet and simple Gospel promise, whosoever shall call on the name of the Lord shall be saved.

Amen and Amen

15 Sixty years in Christ:
a personal testimony

A SERMON PREACHED ON 29TH MAY, 1992 IN THE MARTYRS MEMORIAL CHURCH ON THE SIXTIETH ANNIVERSARY OF HIS CONVERSION TO CHRIST. THE TEXT WAS PSALM 66:16 "COME AND HEAR, ALL YE THAT FEAR GOD, AND I WILL DECLARE WHAT HE HATH DONE FOR MY SOUL."

TURN IN YOUR BIBLE to the Psalm numbered sixty six and at the verse sixteen: *"Come and hear, all ye that fear God, and I will declare what He hath done for my soul."*

Sixty years ago on the twenty-ninth day of May, Nineteen Hundred and Thirty-Two Christ sought me and Christ found me, and I can say today with gladness, rejoicing and praise that Christ has kept me. I want to pay tribute and spell out a testimony this morning to my Saviour and my Lord.

When the great Scottish Reformer John Knox lay dying, he called his wife and said, *"Read me a portion of Holy Writ."* She said, *"Where will I read, John?"* He said, *"Read me in the place where I first cast anchor. Read me the text which brought me to Christ."*

She turned up the seventeenth chapter of John's Gospel and she read to him 'his' text, as he called it: *"And this is eternal life, that we might know Thee the only true God, and Jesus Christ whom Thou hast sent."*

I want today to take you to the text where I first cast my anchor. In Nineteen Hundred and Thirty-two my father was minister of Hill Street Baptist Church in the town of Ballymena. That Church was born out of the great 1859 Revival. It had an unusual parentage. The Covenanting minister of Cullybackey Reformed Presbyterian Church was the Rev. John G. McVicker. He was not a converted man. When the Revival came to the Cullybackey district Mr McVicker was preaching one Sabbath morning and the grace of God touched his soul, and in the pulpit he was gloriously, wonderfully and, praise God, everlastingly converted to Christ. His conversion brought division in his congregation, many of whom did not like it. Consequently he resigned his pastorate.

He went to Ballymena and he built that church in Hill Street.

Every week in that Church my mother held a Children's Meeting. On the twenty-ninth day of May, 1932 that meeting took place as usual. My mother read the scriptures from John chapter twelve and she took for her text verse 11: *"I am the Good Shepherd, the Good Shepherd giveth His life for the sheep"*. The meeting was held in the Lecture Room upstairs at the front of the building.

When the children filed away from that meeting I waited behind. I approached my mother and I told her that as she spoke God had spoken to me. I was lost, and I needed the Good Shepherd to find me and I needed the Good Shepherd to save me. We went downstairs to the church building proper. We went in through the door on the right-hand side and we knelt down at the second pew on the right-hand side of the building. There on that day, as a young lad of six, knowing that I was lost, knowing that in me dwelt no good thing, knowing that nothing could save me but the Blood of Christ and the Saviour Himself, I cast my anchor and, thank God, I cast it on rock solid granite. I cast it upon the impregnable, unchanging, unchangeable, immutable promise of God, that Christ is the Good Shepherd and that He gave His life for the sheep, and because He died I live, and because He shed His Blood my sins were washed away. I came, I tasted, I received. The Bible says, *"Him that cometh I will in no wise cast out."* Mr Nicholson used to say, *"You get many a take-in in life, but what a take-in it is to be taken in to Jesus."* That is the real take-in of life, and, thank God, Christ took me in.

When that Church was being renovated I spoke to its Pastor at the time, and I said, *"What are you going to do with your old pews?"* He said, *"We are going to break them up."* I said, *"Well, I want one of them. I want the pew where I knelt and received Christ."* He said, *"You are welcome to it."* Now I do not believe in relics but I believe in precious memories, and that old pew is down in the Lecture Hall of our College in Banbridge. Recently we had a great Service in that Lecture Hall at eight o'clock in the morning. I got all the students who were there and the Matron and we had an old-fashioned, Holy Ghost praise meeting, and I knelt at that form and I repeated that line,

High Heaven that heard that solemn vow,
That vow renewed shall daily hear,
Till in life's latest hour I bow,
And bless in death a bond so dear.

'COME' - THAT'S AN INVITATION WORD

The Psalmist says, *"Come."* That is an invitation, and what an invitation word it is! All through the Bible that sweet little word *"Come "* is rung out in such pleasing terms and invitations.

The first time it is used in the Bible it is used of Noah. God said to Noah, *"Come into the ark,"* The last time it is used in the Bible is in Revelation chapter 22: 17 *"The Spirit and the Bride say, Come, And let him that heareth say, Come, and let him that is athirst come."* Thank God for this invitation, and I would throw out this invitation to you today, Come, Come, Come, that is the invitation on the lips of Christ to every soul, to every sinful soul. The only qualification you need is to know you are a sinner, and if you know you are a sinner, hear it, Christ did not come to call the righteous. He came to call sinners to repentance. *"They that are whole need not a physician, but they that are sick."*

'HEAR' - THAT'S AN EXHORTATION WORD

Notice the second word: *"Hear."* Well, if *"Come"* is an invitation word, *"Hear"* is an exhortation word. If you look at verse five in the Psalm it reads, *"Come and see,"* but when you look at this text of mine it says, *"Come and hear."* You will notice in verse five it is *"Come and see the terrors of the Lord,* His wrath and His judgment. But, thank God, my text says, "Come and hear the mercy of God, the forgiveness of God."

Do you remember that word in Isaiah? *"Hear and your soul shall live".* Faith cometh by hearing and hearing by the Word of God. How shall they hear without a preacher, and how shall they preach except they be sent?

Before his conversion Hugh Latimer, the great Reformer, was full of zeal but he had no Biblical knowledge. Thomas Bilney - 'Little Bilney,' as he was called among the Reformers because he was small in stature - resolved *"I must reach Hugh Latimer, he needs to hear the Truth."* So he went to Latimer's study and said to Latimer, *"Will you hear my confession?"* Latimer thought he had won a convert from the Protestant faith, and he said, *"Most certainly,"* and Bilney started to tell him what God had done for his soul. Latimer records *"By his confession I learned more than afore in my years, so that from that time forward I began to smell the Word of God, and forsake the School Doctors and such fooleries."*

He began to taste, to smell the Word of God. He heard and his soul did live!

I would exhort you today to hear, not with the hearing of the ear but with the hearing of the heart.

ALL YE THAT FEAR GOD - THAT'S A LIMITATION WORD

"All ye that fear God!" that is a limitation word. There is a limit here. He does not say 'Everyone', he says 'All ye that fear God'. This audience is limited although it is large enough for it includes everyone that fears God. *"The fear of God is the beginning of wisdom,"* and all who have the beginning of God's fear should hear.

Those who do not fear God are blind, they are walking in the blindness of the mystery of iniquity and not in the wisdom of the mystery of godliness. Those who have the fear of God in their heart have loosened feet, they can come. Those who have the fear of God in their heart have opened ears, they can hear. "Come and hear, all ye that fear God."

'I WILL DECLARE' - THAT'S A PROCLAMATION WORD

Notice that the Psalmist had made up his mind that he was going to tell it out. The great sadness of our churches today is that they are largely silent. Commenting on that Scripture I have just quoted to you: *"The Spirit and the Bride say, Come."* One of the old Puritans said, *"Alas, the Bride of Christ is a dumb bride."* The Church is dumb. It is not saying to sinners, *"Come."* It is not saying to sinners *"Come and hear."* It is not declaring to sinners the great things that God has done for its soul. The psalmist made up his mind that he was going to tell it out, that nothing was going to stop him. He was going to give God the glory. He was going to honour his Saviour. He was going to emphasise that it was by the grace of God he was what he was.

C.H. Spurgeon said, *"Let no mock modesty restrain the grateful believer from speaking of himself, or rather of God's dealings to himself, for that is justly due to God. Neither let him shun the individual use of the first person. Let him not be afraid to say 'I have a personal testimony to what God has done for my soul. It is correct in detailing the Lord's way of love to use the first person. We are not to be egotists but in our Christian testimony we must be egotists when we witness*

for the Lord. We must be able to tell, not someone else's experience but our personal, living, up-to-date experience with Jesus Christ."
Things will happen when the church recovers that.

Could I ask you a question? When last did you give a personal testimony to any person about what God has done for your soul? Just ask yourself the question.

D.L. Moody vowed he would never let a day pass without telling someone about the Lord Jesus. One day he went to his room and the Spirit of God convicted him and said, "You did not do it today." So as he went out into the rain. There was a man walking and he had his umbrella up and Moody joined him. Thank God, he witnessed to him of the blessed joy of salvation, and the witness was effectual. I tell you, my friend, we should be delighted to tell men of what God has done for our souls. *"I will declare what He hath done for my soul". I will declare, that is a proclamation. He makes up his mind, "I will declare. I am not going to let anybody stop me. They may think I am a fool, a headcase, an idiot or anything else, but I am going to let them know, I will declare."* That is a proclamation.

'HE HATH DONE FOR MY SOUL' - THAT'S A TRANSFORMATION WORD

Let us look at the last word: *"What He hath done for my soul ."* That is a transformation word. Every person who talks about the Lord, who is redeemed and converted and saved by God's grace, has to talk about what God has done for his own soul.

Old Timothy Rodgers, one of the great Puritan preachers who lived from 1660 to 1729, said: *"After we are delivered from the dreadful apprehensions of the wrath of God, it is our duty to publicly thank God. It is for the glory of our Healer to speak of those miserable wounds that once pained us, and of the kind hand that saved us when we were brought so very low. It is for the glory of our Pilot to tell of the rocks and of the sands, the many dangers and threatening calamities that He by His wise conduct made us to escape, and to see us safe on the shore. That will cause others that are still afflicted, and others that are tossed with tempest to look to Jesus for help, for if He was able to save you He can save them. If He was able to deliver you He can deliver them. We must, like soldiers when the war is over and the battle finished, relate our combats, our fears, our dangers, with delight and make known our experiences to doubting, troubled Christians, and to those who have not yet been under such laws and severe trials as we have been under."* What words of wisdom!

The best way to comfort a storm-tossed soul is to tell how you were comforted in the storm. The best way to bring healing to a sin-stricken soul is to tell how God brought healing to your heart, and comfort through the application of that marvellous remedy - the Precious, Precious Blood of the Lamb - What He has done for my soul!

ONE: HE WROUGHT MY SOUL

We should thank God, first of all, that God has in His goodness wrought our soul. It was a curious wroughting, was it not?

Look at verse 16 of Psalm 139: *"Thine eyes did see my substance, yet being unperfect; and in thy book all my members were written, which in continuance were fashioned, when as yet there was none of them."* The fifteenth verse says: *"My substance was not hid from Thee, when I was made in secret, and curiously **wrought** in the lowest parts of the earth."*

What a wroughting that was when God wrought our soul and our body as it was formed in our mother's womb! He saw to it that we came forth with life. Our birth was to life and not to death. I am amazed, as I read the Scriptures, at the wonder of God's eternal plan. Long before time began I was part of God's plan. Before the hills in order stood or earth received her frame, He has wrought my soul! Let me tell you what God has done for my soul.

TWO: HE SOUGHT MY SOUL

He did something else, then, thank God, He sought my soul. And what a seeking that was! It meant that long journey, the longest of all journeys that ever was taken - a journey from Eternity into time. No one can imagine the chasm which separates Eternity from time. Only God, the Eternal God could bridge that chasm. Praise God, the Eternal Word became flesh and dwelt among us, Why? He was seeking for our soul. All that long, long way He came! I will tell you what He has done for my soul, He wrought it, He sought it.

THREE: HE BOUGHT MY SOUL

Bless God, He bought it. Yonder at Calvary with thorn-crowned brow and nail-pierced hand and back ploughed with the awful scourging, He bought it.

There He voluntarily burst His heart and let His Blood flow. He had power to lay it down, and lay it down He did willingly, voluntarily. "No man taketh it from me."

It was not the pangs inflicted by man, or the wrath poured on Him by God which took away his Life. It was His own voluntary surrender of His Life for me. The spear did not cause the Blood to be shed, the spear simply opened the pericardium around the heart to prove that all the Blood of the heart had already been shed in that act of atonement which the Lord Jesus did for me at Calvary.

"Was it for me He bowed His head
Upon that Cross and freely shed
His Precious Blood, that Crimson Tide
Was it for me my Saviour died?"

Blessed be God I can say, "It was for me, Yes all for me." Can you say that? "It was for me"?

I will tell you what things He hath done for my soul: He wrought it, He sought it, He bought it.

FOUR: HE BROUGHT MY SOUL

And, praise God, He brought it. The old lost sheep was brought home. He laid it on His shoulders and He brought it home. Oh, what a great day when God brings a sinner home to the place of pardon and the place of peace! The Scotsman said: *"It's better felt than telt."* And so it is! Oh, the joy, the glory, the wonder, the transport, the rapture of a soul that is put into Christ forever! *"I give unto my sheep eternal life, and they shall never perish."* The Good Shepherd giveth His Life for the sheep.

In John's Gospel chapter ten you will notice: *"My sheep hear my voice,"* that is the mystery of mysteries.

A Gospel meeting takes place, the general call of the Gospel goes out and men pass it by, but somewhere in a pew there sits a man, there sits a woman, and the sheep hear His voice and they follow Him.

I am glad that that mystery was fulfilled in my life and I recognised on the twenty-ninth day of May, 1932 the voice of the Good Shepherd. The Voice! *"He drew me and I followed on, charmed to confess the voice Divine."*

What a Charmer is the Lord Jesus Christ when He charms a soul away from sin and away from the world, and away from Hell into His living embrace, into the grace of the Blessed Son of God! Do you know anything about it? *"Charmed to confess that voice Divine."*

FIVE: HE GOT MY SOUL

Last of all, can I say humbly and with joy in my heart, He not only wrought it and sought it, and bought it and brought it, but, thank God, He has got it. He has got my soul. He has got it today. It is His.

Do you remember what Paul says? *"I know Whom I have believed, and am persuaded that He is able to keep that which I have committed unto Him against that day."*

I am not my own, He has got me! Salvation does not make you miserable, it makes you merry. Salvation does not make you sad, it makes you glad.

Billy Bray, the Cornish saint, said, *"Once I was a bad man and a sad man. God however made me a glad man. The world said I was a madman, But God and I know I am a glad man."*

Oh, let me tell you there is a gladness in Jesus Christ! "Come" that is an invitation word. "Hear" that is an exhortation word. "All ye that fear God" that is a limitation word. "And I will declare" that is a declaration word. "What God hath done for my soul" that is a transformation word. Oh, dear sinner, meet Jesus Christ today!

A big man was in the gospel hour last Sunday night. He walked through the door into the Kirk Session room and he said, *"You gave me good news, preacher tonight. You told me I could get all my sins forgiven and go home without any of them."* I said, *"You got the message,"* and down on his knees he fell and said, *"Oh, God, forgive my sins, pardon me, save me."*

God's salvation, that is what men need today. You know if we kept talking about it and telling it, hundreds, thousands would come to Jesus, but we are silent.

May God save us from being a bunch of dummies, and may God give us a trumpet to blow, a testimony to give and a shout to raise for the gospel of Jesus Christ.

Acts 5: 42 *"And daily in the temple, and in every house, they ceased not to teach and preach Jesus Christ."*

Amen and Amen